Praise for *Leadership & Sustai*

Leadership & Sustainability *extends and amplifies Fullan's thinking in very powerful and practical ways, by developing a topic that hasn't seen this kind of elegant, integrative, and comprehensive treatment before. It uses real-world examples and research literature to tackle, head on, the question of sustainability—how organizations move into the future and endure over time, as well as the equally challenging question: What about an organization is worth sustaining long term? Folks who have followed Michael Fullan's work over many years will like this book very much.*

Richard Ackerman
Associate Professor, Educational Leadership
The University of Maine
Co-Director, The International Network
of Principal's Center, Harvard University

An ambitious and provocative journey into the complexities and possibilities that arise when leadership and sustainability join.

Roland S. Barth
Author

Leadership & Sustainability *is a critical breakthrough. Michael Fullan has utilized findings from some of the best research and observations in education over the past 15 years to brilliantly illuminate the challenges of creating schools capable of continuous organic change and improvement.*

James P. Comer
Maurice Falk Professor of Child Psychiatry
Yale Child Study Center, Yale University

Michael Fullan has gone beyond his past research that described the change process so insightfully to a new and exciting exploration of how systems thinking and the "long lever of leadership" can bring about deep and lasting reforms in schools and schooling. This brand of leadership for sustainability, as described by Fullan, results in the "deep learning" that enables schools to respond successfully to the revolution in expectations they now face. This new work will both inform and inspire educators to become the "new theoreticians" whose impact will be felt in their schools every day.

David T. Conley
Associate Professor, Educational Leadership and Policy
Director, Center for Educational Policy Research
College of Education, University of Oregon

With knowledgeable savvy from both individual leadership and system transformation, and a knack for writing in "plain-speak," Fullan helps us understand that it will be "leadership" (not leaders) that pave the way for great sustainability. His attempt to link abstract concepts to concrete examples of what it looks like in practice was successful.

Theodore B. Creighton
Director, Center for Research and Doctoral Studies
Sam Houston State University
Executive Director, National Council
of Professors of Education Administration

Efforts at education reform have taken us down a variety of paths, and Michael Fullan has consistently noted the importance of leadership to large-scale reform. In his latest book, Leadership & Sustainability, *Fullan makes a solid case that such reform is a complex process involving many variables. Key among these variables is the relationship between leadership and sustainability.*

Vincent L. Ferrandino
Executive Director
National Association of Elementary School Principals
Alexandria, Virginia

Michael Fullan has been among the most salient international observers of educational change over the past decade. In this book, he draws upon a diverse knowledge base in a critical examination of the limitations of current education reform strategies in use around the world. He then answers his own challenge by seeking to identify what it will take to create sustainable educational reform. His approach will be of interest to a broad range of educational leaders, policy makers, and scholars.

Philip Hallinger
Executive Director
College of Management
Mahidol University
Bangkok, Thailand

While everyone is debating quick-fix reform in education, Michael Fullan sets out a compelling strategy for widespread and lasting improvement. Drawing on experience from around the world and examples at every level, Fullan brilliantly personifies the transformative theorist-in-action that he urges others to be. This book is essential. Don't leave school without it!

Andy Hargreaves
Thomas More Brennan
Chair in Education
Lynch School of Education
Boston College

In Leadership & Sustainability, *Michael Fullan continues to push the edge of what we understand about improving schools on a large scale. His ideas, both provocative and practical, are well worth the attention of educational reformers, policy makers, and practitioners alike.*

Kenneth A. Leithwood
Professor and Associate Dean
Ontario Institute for Studies in Education
University of Toronto

No one has contributed more to our understanding of leadership and change than Michael Fullan. Leadership & Sustainability *continues that tradition—a brilliant analysis of a timely topic.*

Thomas J. Sergiovanni
Lillian Radford Professor of Education
Trinity University
San Antonio, TX

Michael Fullan does it again—providing yet another significant resolve to educational leadership. In an era marked by changing demographics, increased accountability, and a wave of anticipated retirements, Fullan offers a vision and a road map for designing and implementing strategies that can result in systemic reform in our nation's schools.

Gerald N. Tirozzi
Executive Director
National Association of Secondary School Principals
Reston, Virginia

Michael Fullan has produced another powerful and inspirational book. He has the wonderful knack of continually positioning himself a couple of steps ahead of the fields. By so doing, he is able to challenge and lead thinking and thereby accelerate productive new developments.

David Hopkins
Head of Standards and Effectiveness Unit
Department for Education and Skills, England

Fullan displays his usual and unique capacity to explain the complexity for improving schools and school systems. He provides vivid examples that illuminate the pathways for head teachers, policy makers and academics wishing to combine immediate results with long-term and greater benefits. Fullan's books—and this is no exception—are for educational policy makers, practitioners, and researchers what J. K. Rowling's Harry Potter books are for children and parents. This is one of the best and most useful.

Tim Brighouse
London Leadership Centre
London, England

leadership & sustainability

System Thinkers
in Action

Michael Fullan

A Joint Publication

CORWIN PRESS

ONTARIO
PRINCIPALS'
COUNCIL
Exemplary Leadership
in Public Education

CORWIN PRESS
A Sage Publications Company
Thousand Oaks, California

For information:

Corwin Press
A Sage Publications Company
2455 Teller Road
Thousand Oaks, California 91320
www.corwinpress.com

Sage Publications Ltd.
1 Oliver's Yard
55 City Road
London EC1Y 1SP
United Kingdom

Sage Publications India Pvt. Ltd.
B-42, Panchsheel Enclave
Post Box 4109
New Delhi 110 017 India

Printed in the United States of America

Library of Congress Cataloging-in-Publication Data

Leadership & sustainability: System thinkers in action / Michael Fullan.
    p. cm.
Includes bibliographical references and index.
ISBN 1-4129-0495-1 — ISBN 1-4129-0496-X (pbk.)
    1. School management and organization—England. 2. Educational change—England.
3. Educational leadership—England. I. Title: Leadership and sustainability. II. Title.
LB2901.F85 2005
371.2′00941—dc22   2004010042

This book is printed on acid-free paper.

        05   06   10   9   8   7   6   5

Acquisitions Editor:	Robert D. Clouse
Editorial Assistant:	Jingle Vea
Production Editor:	Diane S. Foster
Copy Editor:	Carla Freeman
Typesetter:	C&M Digitals (P) Ltd.
Proofreader:	Taryn Bigelow
Indexer:	Julie Grayson
Cover Designer:	Tracy E. Miller
Graphic Designer:	Anthony Paular

Contents

Preface

All the dilemmas in education reform are coming home to roost: top-down versus bottom-up; short-term versus long-term results; centralization versus decentralization; informed prescription versus informed professional judgment; transactional versus transformative leadership; excellence versus equity. And how does one achieve large-scale reform, anyway; reform that is characterized by serious accountability and ownership?

As it turns out, "sustainability" is at the heart of all these dilemmas. Its definition is not straightforward. It is not how to maintain good programs beyond implementation. It is not how to keep going in a linear, sustained fashion. It is not how to keep up relentless energy. For the moment, let's be satisfied with a general definition: *Sustainability is the capacity of a system to engage in the complexities of continuous improvement consistent with deep values of human purpose.* There is a lot packed into this definition. It is not just the outcome of continuous improvement we need to observe, but we must also understand the key characteristics of systems that display dynamic sustainability.

My thanks in particular to my colleague, Andy Hargreaves, who has been working on the concept of sustainability over the last several years. His definition overlaps but is different from mine. As he and Fink put it: "Sustainability does not simply mean whether something will last. It addresses how particular initiatives can be developed without compromising the development of others in the surrounding environment now and in the future" (Hargreaves & Fink, 2000, p. 30; Hargreaves & Fink, in press).

I focus not so much on particular initiatives but on the system itself. My concern is not just whether system thinking is important (Senge, 1990). It is. Rather, I tackle a question that has never been addressed before: How do you develop and sustain a greater number of "system thinkers in action." I call this breed of leader "the new theoretician." These are leaders at all levels of the system who proactively and naturally take into account and interact with larger parts of the system as they bring about deeper reform and help produce other leaders working on the same issues. They are theoreticians, but they are practitioners whose theories are lived in action every day. In fact, that is what makes their impact so powerful. Their ideas are woven into daily interactions that make a difference.

The agenda for the new theoreticians is laid out in Chapter 2 as eight elements of sustainability: public service with a moral purpose, commitment to changing the context, lateral capacity building, intelligent accountability, deep learning, dual commitment to short- and long-term results, cyclical energizing, and the long lever of leadership. The agenda is exceedingly complex and demanding. I show specifically why it will be hard to accomplish. But I also show what the new work looks like in practice, because it is now going on. This book is about identifying what leaders at all levels of the system can do to pave the way for greater sustainability.

One other matter. We are getting into complex territory. I undertake in the book, as the new theoreticians do in practice, to link every abstract concept with a concrete example of what it looks like in practice. You can't be a system thinker in action if you don't know what the action part looks like and feels like. Learning by doing has never been so thoughtful and so challenging.

The revolution I am talking about is under way in all of the public services: education, health, employment, transportation, crime, and in business, for that matter. As agencies have pushed for greater performance and public accountability over the past two decades, we have seen some incremental improvements, but it is obvious that these improvements are fragile and not deep. But we are reluctant to let go of the strategies that have brought us this far, in favor of strategies that are far more complex with many more unknowns. In this book, my goal is to portray where we are in public service reform, with education as the main example, and to outline how we might pursue longer-term sustainability without jeopardizing short-term results. Indeed, the public will insist on this reconciliation.

In the systems level work, I have benefited enormously from my association with Michael Barber, head of the Prime Minister's Policy Delivery Unit in Britain. Michael is one of the great theoreticians in action that I write about in this book.

Leadership (not "leaders") is the key to the new revolution. This book is about the two-way street between individual leadership and system transformation. They must feed on each other in a virtual cycle, even though at any given time they may be asymmetrical; that is, individual leaders in a given instance may find the system is less than helpful, and in another circumstance, system leaders may find individual leaders to be stumbling blocks to improvement. In any case, leadership is to this decade what standards were to the 1990s if we want large-scale, sustainable reform.

In education, the many initiatives in large-scale reform over the past decade have provided the foundation for challenging the future. We understand (and will review) what brought us incremental success in, for example, districtwide reform, as when the performance of most schools in the district improve. By looking closely, we can also see why the strategies that brought us initial success cannot take us the distance.

My colleagues and I have been fortunate to be partners, codevelopers, critical-friend observers of several significant large-scale reform initiatives around the world, but especially in Canada, the United Kingdom, the United States, and Australia. The ideas, translated into many languages, are in use around the globe, not only in education, but in the public service more broadly as well as in the corporate world.

We have learned a great deal from our evaluation of the National Literacy and Numeracy Strategies in England and now, in the aftermath in the more fundamental policy work, to go beyond improvements in literacy and numeracy.

My special appreciation to David Miliband, David Hopkins, and the scores of educators in England at all levels who are providing us with a living laboratory of educational reform on a grand scale. Thanks also to David Hopkins for very helpful comments on the manuscript.

In the United States, the work in Chicago; Greensboro, North Carolina; and in Louisiana with the Center for Development and Learning is producing powerful lessons about districtwide reform (as well as the research literature more broadly on district reform). My association with the Gates Foundation Leadership initiative, and now Microsoft's Partnership in Learning, adds significantly to the laboratories of large-scale reform.

I have been privileged over this past year to be the H. Smith Richardson Jr. Visiting Fellow at the Center for Creative Leadership

(CCL) in Greensboro, North Carolina. John Alexander and his colleagues at CCL have been an inspiration to work with in pushing the boundaries of new work on leadership.

In Canada, districtwide reform initiatives in Edmonton Catholic District, Toronto School District, and more recently and deeply, York Region School District are great examples of building system capacity. In Ontario as a whole, with the recent election of the Liberal government, we have a golden opportunity to swim in deeper waters as the Premier, Dalton McGuinty, and the Minister of Education, Gerard Kennedy commit to provincewide reform based on many of the ideas in this book.

In Australia, we are in the early stages of significant system level developments in the state of South Australia as the state has committed to system redesign, again based on the new work of capacity building. Virtually all of the states in Australia have started down the path of large-scale reform.

My point is not to limit the observations to these cases, but to say that these are only some of the ones where we have direct involvement. They are part and parcel of the larger revolution. I will also argue that it would be easy to fall back on strategies that are getting some short-term results, but this would be a fundamental mistake. The new breakthroughs are complex and sophisticated, and will require leaders who have more comprehensive conceptualization than most leaders of the present (more accurately, systems have not fostered and permitted the development of such leadership).

The new knowledge, as I have said, is being led not by academic theoreticians; the new theoreticians are certain policymakers and lead practitioners working with a wider set of ideas and interacting with academics who themselves are immersed in practical theorizing and doing. This is crucial because it means the ideas and strategies are being formed around real problems—big ones never before solved. Never before have we had such a change crucible at our fingertips.

In many ways, this book builds on the ideas that were set out in what I have come to call the "ad hoc trilogy on leadership." *Leading in a Culture of Change* (2001) demonstrated that successful leaders in education and business have much in common. The five core mind-action sets—moral purpose, understanding change processes, relationship building, knowledge building, and coherence making—characterize successful leaders in all learning organizations, that is, all organizations operating in complex times.

In *Change Forces With a Vengeance* (2003a), I advocated the tri-level reform model, namely, what has to happen at the school/community, district, and state levels, and in their interactions across levels. We will see that concerted tri-level developments are central to system transformation, to changing the very contexts within which people work.

In *The Moral Imperative of School Leadership* (2003b), I took the ideas further by arguing that not only must moral purpose guide and drive our efforts, but moral purpose must also go beyond individual heroism to the level of a system quality.

What is exciting is that there are new, fundamental attempts at systems thinking, strategizing, and doing that give us much more to think about and build on—again, the purpose of this book.

I would be remiss if I did not say that we could identify examples that are mired in the old pattern of incremental inertia at best and compliant dependency at worst. At their extremes, incremental inertia and sustainability are mutually exclusive. However, I will argue that it is possible, and necessary, to pursue a dual strategy that pays attention to short-term results while simultaneously laying the groundwork for sustainable engagement. We need to have our cake and eat it, too.

I thank Robb Clouse of Corwin Press, who is constantly pushing the envelope; the Ontario Principals' Council for its entrepreneurial leadership and support; and Claudia Cuttress for producing this book, and the many training materials and books that have fed into it, all with amazing quality and speed.

I dedicate this book to the new theoreticians—doers with big minds, who treat moral purpose as a cognitive as well as an emotional calling.

To the New Theoreticians:
Doers With Big Minds

About the Author

 **Michael Fullan** is the former Dean of the Ontario Institute for Studies in Education of the University of Toronto. He is recognized as an international authority on education reform. He is engaged in training in, consulting for, and evaluating change projects around the world. His ideas for managing change are used in many countries, and his books have been published in several languages. His books, which are widely acclaimed, include *What's Worth Fighting For* trilogy (with Andy Hargreaves), *Change Forces* trilogy, *The New Meaning of Educational Change,* and *Leading in a Culture of Change* that was awarded the 2002 Book of the Year Award by the National Staff Development Council. His latest books are *Change Forces With a Vengeance,* completing the *Change Forces* trilogy, and *The Moral Imperative of School Leadership.* In April 2004, he was appointed Special Adviser on Education to the Premier, and Minister of Education in Ontario.

CHAPTER ONE

The Starting Point

So hope for a great sea-change. . . .
It means once in a lifetime that justice can rise up
And hope and history rhyme.

—Seamus Heaney

W here are we in large-scale reform? It is a bit unfair to characterize the best success as incremental inertia, but in terms of sustainability, that label is not too far off the mark. In the first part of this chapter, I consider examples of large-scale reform that have been successful, concluding that progress has been made but that it is neither deep nor sustainable. I also identify some reasons why we should be concerned about the inadequacies of these strategies.

APPARENT SUCCESS

Nearly all of the success stories involve improvements in literacy and numeracy at the elementary level, with some closing of the gap between high- and low-performing schools. The findings are consistent across many studies. Togneri and Anderson's (2003) study of success in five high-poverty districts identified six strategies for improvement. These districts

1. Acknowledged publicly poor performance and sought solutions (building the will for reform)

2. Focused intensively on improving instruction and achievement

3. Built a systemwide framework and infrastructure to support instruction

4. Redefined and redistributed leadership at all levels of the district

5. Made professional development relevant and useful

6. Recognized there were no quick fixes. (p. 13)

In another study of four successful high-poverty districts, Snipes, Doolittle, and Herlihy (2002) found that these districts in comparison with other districts

1. Focused on achievement, standards, and instructional practice

2. Created concrete accountability systems in relation to results

3. Focused on the lowest-performing schools

4. Adopted districtwide curricular and instructional approaches

5. Established districtwide professional development and support for consistent implementation

6. Drove reform into the classrooms by defining the role for central offices of guiding, supporting, and improving instruction at the building level

7. Committed themselves to data-driven decision making and instruction

8. Started the reform at the elementary level

9. Provided intensive instruction in reading and math to middle and high schools students. (p. 5)

Similarly, and at a more operational school level, a study by the Council of Chief School Officers (2002) found that school principals who were successful employed nine improvement strategies by

1. Setting high expectations for all students

2. Sharing leadership and staying engaged

3. Encouraging collaboration among staff

4. Using assessment data to support student success

5. Keeping the focus on students

6. Addressing barriers to learning

7. Reinforcing classroom learning at home

8. Employing systems for identifying interventions

9. Defining special education as the path to success in the general education program. (p. 8)

In all of the above cases, leadership at the school and district levels was identified as crucial to success. As consistent as these findings seem, there are many problems with them, but let us first consider other large-scale reforms.

The most celebrated case of large-scale reform is the National Literacy and Numeracy Strategies (NLNS) in England. We had the privilege of evaluating the strategy over a 5-year period, from 1997 to 2002 (Earl, Levin, Leithwood, Fullan, & Watson, 2003). The main elements of the implementation strategy were summarized by Michael Barber (2002), head of the government initiative:

- A nationally prepared project plan for both literacy and numeracy, setting out actions, responsibilities, and deadlines through to 2002
- A substantial investment sustained over at least 6 years and skewed toward those schools that need most help
- A project infrastructure involving national direction from the Standards and Effectiveness Unit, 15 regional directors, and over 300 expert consultants at the local level for each of the two strategies

- An expectation that every class will have a daily math lesson and daily literacy hour
- A detailed teaching programme covering every school year for children from ages 5 to 11
- An emphasis on early intervention and catch-up for pupils who fall behind
- A professional development programme designed to enable every primary school teacher to learn to understand and use proven best practices in both curriculum areas
- The appointment of over 2,000 leading math teachers and hundreds of expert literacy teachers who have the time and skill to model best practice for their peers
- The provision of "intensive support" to circa half of all schools where the most progress is required
- A major investment in books for schools (over 23 million new books in the system since May 1997)
- The removal of barriers to implementation (especially a huge reduction in prescribed curriculum content outside the core subjects)
- Regular monitoring and extensive evaluation by our national inspection agency, OFSTED
- A national curriculum for initial teacher training requiring all providers to prepare new primary schoolteachers to teach the daily math lesson and the literacy hour
- A problem-solving philosophy involving early identification of difficulties as they emerge and the provision of rapid solutions or intervention where necessary
- The provision of extra after school, weekend, and holiday booster classes for those who need extra help to reach the standard. (pp. 8–9)

England used a combination of "pressure and support," or what we now call "accountability and capacity building," to mobilize leadership for literacy and mathematics. New literacy and math leadership roles were established at the school, district, regional, and national levels and later were supplemented by direct professional development for school principals and initial teacher education. So, leadership was central to success. Capacity building involves developing the collective ability—dispositions, skills, knowledge, motivation, and resources—to act together to bring about positive change.

Figure 1.1   Results of School Reform in England (Department for Education and Skills, 2004)

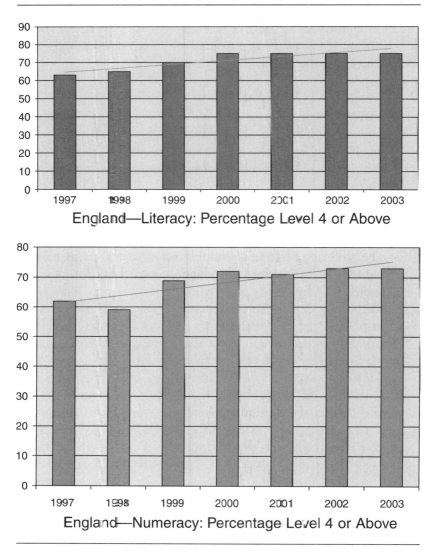

England—Literacy: Percentage Level 4 or Above

England—Numeracy: Percentage Level 4 or Above

The results were impressive, but tell two stories. Using 11-year-olds as the marker, Figure 1.1 shows the percentage of pupils achieving proficiency (Levels 4 and 5 in the English system).

First, the results are remarkable. Within a 4-year period (1997–2000), literacy and math proficiency increased from slightly over 60% to about 75%. This in 20,000 schools! Second, performance plateaued in 2000 and has remained at that level for the past 3 years even though the initial strategy has become, if anything, more sophisticated.

Before throwing one more spanner into the works, let's take critical stock. First, by focusing directly on literacy and mathematics with appropriate pressure and support, one can get a boost of improvement.

Second, even with enormous effort, there is only a minority of schools and districts deeply engaged in these strategies, especially if we use "closing the gap" as the main criterion.

Third, the results plateau well below acceptable levels. After a sharp increase between 1997 and 2000, the results have remained at the same level for the past 3 years.

Fourth, are even the good results sustainable? In a word, NO. The strategies have required tremendous energy and supervision, which in their own right cannot be sustained for long (burnout, turnover, overload take their toll). Related to this, motivation to continue was evident as long as results were improving; what happens when improvement plateaus and it takes the same great effort just to stand still? There is no chance that the strategies described to this point could result in widespread, sustainable reform.

Fifth, do the results represent deep learning? There is no indication that "engagement of students in learning" has significantly increased just because there are more students who can read and are numerate. Advances in cognitive science and in what citizens of the future need in a complex, global society show how deep the learning must be. Guy Claxton's (2002) framework of *Building Learning Power* is a case in point:

> Developing learning power means working on four aspects of student learning. The first task is to help them become more *resilient:* able to lock onto learning and to resist distractions either from outside or within. The second is helping them become more *resourceful:* able to draw on a wide range of learning methods and strategies as appropriate. The third is building the ability to be *reflective:* to think profitably about learning and themselves as learners. And the fourth task is to make them capable of being *reciprocal:* making use of relationships in the most productive, enjoyable and responsible way. (p. 17; emphasis in original)

David Hargreaves (2003) also makes the point that the school curriculum is seriously out of step with what is needed in present and future society, where new knowledge and skills are at a premium:

> The ability to learn how to learn and other meta-cognitive or "thinking" skills; the ability to learn on the job and in teams; the ability to cope with ambiguous situations and unpredictable problems; the ability to communicate well verbally, not just in writing; and the ability to be creative, innovative, and entrepreneurial. (p. 30)

Similarly, Bereiter (2002) argues forcefully that we need far deeper learning than hitherto imagined for both students and teachers. Indeed as we shall see, "deep learning" is one of the eight elements of sustainability.

Sixth, and finally, note that in all cases, the strategy is heavily centrally directed at the district or state levels (one group above proudly claimed that it "drove reforms into the classrooms"). Soon, we will see that centrally driven reforms can be a necessary first start (when performance is seriously unacceptable) but can never carry the day of sustainability.

To nudge our thinking in the direction of sustainability, I take Michael Barber's response to the fact that an apparently successful strategy was plateauing. Figure 1.2 displays the framework he used to characterize the evolution of needed strategies for reform.

Barber (2002) argued that some conditions for reform can be described on a continuum from "knowledge poor" (quality knowledge is not being generated and accessed on an ongoing basis) to "knowledge rich." The other dimension is whether the strategy is centrally driven or is based on local capacity or judgment. The result is a helpful (but an incomplete) transition toward a sustainability paradigm. Interpreting the figure itself, we can say there was a time when teachers worked autonomously "behind the classroom door" (there is still much of that). As a loosely coupled *system,* it can be described as "uninformed professional judgment." There were some excellent teachers, but there was no culture in place to systematically extend and deepen quality teaching.

As anxiety about the performance of schools became more public in the 1980s—think "A Nation at Risk" in the United States—new accountability schemes were introduced, but these were not

Figure 1.2   Knowledge Poor Versus Rich, Prescription Versus
Judgment Matrix

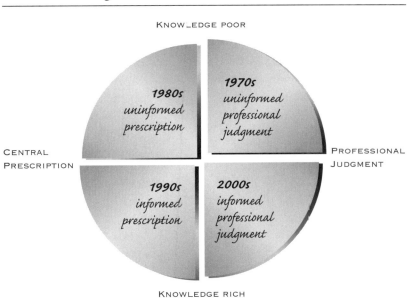

KNOWLEDGE POOR

	1980s *uninformed* *prescription*	*1970s* *uninformed* *professional* *judgment*
CENTRAL PRESCRIPTION		PROFESSIONAL JUDGMENT
	1990s *informed* *prescription*	*2000s* *informed* *professional* *judgment*

KNOWLEDGE RICH

SOURCE: Barber, 2002.

based on sound or comprehensive knowledge: hence, uninformed prescription.

As evidence accumulated about how to improve student achievement (both with respect to curriculum and instruction and in terms of change strategies), some jurisdictions locked on to a more centrally driven (and supported) set of strategies. They did their homework, with the result being "informed prescription." England's NLNS is a prime example. Barber (2002), then, acknowledges that such prescription, no matter how wise, cannot solve the leveling-off problem. To go beyond initial plateauing, one needs a great deal of "informed professional judgment."

For my own part, it is important to clarify from the work on professional learning communities that informed professional judgment must be understood to be a *collective* quality, not just an individual one (i.e., groups of teachers and others create a system of ongoing collective deliberation and development); and it must have strong *external* connections to the wider environment of knowledge, not just collaboration within. Furthermore, such cultures are not particularly congenial; they are demanding cultures as people continually press for better results.

Still, there is a larger dilemma. In an era of urgency and accountability, what happens if you invest in and give over to informed professional judgment but it turns out the group does not have the *capacity* (resources, skills, culture) to act effectively? Won't such an investment drift into uninformed judgment? As we move toward sustainability in the next section, we need to keep this tension in mind. It is the classic centralization-decentralization dilemma. Any solution that aspires toward sustainability must reconcile this dilemma.

DANGER POINTS

I said there was one more spanner, and it comes in the form of an intriguing book by a professor of management, William Ouchi (2003). The gist of what I am going to end up saying is that in the press to do what's best for students and in the complexity of so doing, it is easy to get the strategy wrong, especially when it comes to learning lessons from examples of apparent success.

In *Making Schools Work* (Ouchi, 2003), the main argument is presented as follows:

> Ouchi's 2001–2002 study examined innovative school systems in Edmonton (Canada), Seattle, and Houston, and compared them with the three largest traditional school systems: New York, Los Angeles, and Chicago. Researchers discovered that the schools that consistently performed best also had the most decentralized management systems, in which autonomous principals—not administrators in a central office—controlled school budgets and personnel hiring policies. They were fully responsible and fully accountable for the performance of their schools. With greater freedom and flexibility to shape their educational programs, hire specialists as needed, and generally determine the direction of their school, the best principals will act as entrepreneurs, says Ouchi. Those who do poorly are placed under the supervision of successful principals, who assume responsibility for the failing schools. (Dust jacket copy)

Using standard achievement tests, Ouchi (2003) shows that schools in the three innovative districts have moved ahead in their own right and in relation to the comparison districts. It is also the case, as Ouchi acknowledges, that many schools are not moving forward.

Ouchi (2003) then proceeds to reveal the "seven keys to success." What is called for, he says, "is to uproot the existing top-down way of doing things and replace it with huge, revolutionary change" (pp. 13–14). The seven keys to success are

1. Every principal is an entrepreneur.

2. Every school controls its own budget.

3. Everyone is accountable for student performance and for budgets.

4. Everyone delegates authority to those below.

5. There is a burning focus on student achievement.

6. Every school is a community of learners.

7. Families have real choices among a variety of unique schools. (p. 14)

There are two issues for me. One is the problem of misinterpreting the lessons; the other is the unlikelihood that the model itself will produce sustainability. Relative to the former, to the extent Ouchi is on the right track, those looking at the lessons might get the message wrong. There is a growing problem in large-scale reform; namely, the *terms* travel well, but the underlying *conceptualization and thinking* do not.

This is an age-old issue in knowledge dissemination. There is a great deal of tacit and in-depth contextual knowledge that would be required to understand the lessons at work. For example, one could easily conclude that site-based management or decentralization is the answer. Ouchi, in fact, claims that both top-down and bottom-up energies are required. Furthermore, issues of holding people accountable and building communities of learners within and across scores of schools are enormously complex.

The second matter concerns doubts about whether the model can work on a large, sustainable scale. Ouchi does not use the terms *capacity* or *capacity building* in his entire book. They are not in the index. And autonomy to act is not the same thing as capacity. There is no chance that large-scale reform will happen, let alone stick, unless capacity building is a central component of the strategy for improvement. Related to this, we now know that capacity building *throughout the system* at all levels must be developed in concert, and to do this will require powerful new system forces. Finally, for the system as a whole to change (a key part of my sustainability argument), you must have school and district leaders who are committed to interacting laterally with other schools and districts in order to learn from each other and to identify with the larger purpose of educational reform.

Failure to act in this direction will result in continued crude or incomplete attempts at large-scale reform, which makes little difference while wasting enormous energy. U.S. President George W. Bush's No Child Left Behind (NCLB) reform act is a case in point. NCLB requires all states to have an achievement-driven system in which "annual yearly progress" in student achievement is documented and reported publicly for every school in each state, with a sequence of escalating consequences for those schools not improving. There is little investment in capacity building and it places people in a high-alert dependency mode, jumping from one solution to another in a desperate attempt to comply. Any minor gains are bound to be outweighed by a system that guarantees superficiality, temporary solutions, and cynicism in the face of impossible goals (see Popham, 2004, for a devastating critique of No Child Left Behind).

A more palatable but incomplete example is the decade-long (1990s) experience with whole-school reform models. Whole-school models (Success for All being the most well-known) with proven track records were validated and funded for dissemination to schools and districts interested in adopting the models. The idea was that these high-quality, school-focused solutions would carry the day, but here was a recipe for nonsustainability even when models were well implemented, because of a failure to consider the kind of "whole-system" capacity building that would be required (see Fullan, 2004, for a critique).

In short, we need a radically new mind-set for reconciling the seemingly intractable dilemmas fundamental for sustainable reform: top-down versus bottom-up, local and central accountability, informed prescription and informed professional judgment, improvement that keeps being replenished. We need, in other words, to tackle the problem of sustainability head-on.

CHAPTER TWO

The Intriguing
Nature of Sustainability

As the struggle to achieve large-scale reform evolves, sustainability is becoming a rallying concept, one that contains the elaboration of strategies essential for whole-system capacity building on an ongoing basis. This chapter attempts to lay out the emerging nature of what sustainability is, especially what built-in strategies simultaneously constitute and promote it.

LOOKING FOR SOLUTIONS

The starting point is to observe that nothing tried so far really works. Local autonomy, whether it is the "let a thousand flowers bloom variety" or site-based management within a framework of external accountability, does not produce results on any scale; the command, control, and support strategy of informed prescription takes us some distance, but it is still surface stuff without any likelihood of lasting.

Any solutions must be efficient, sophisticated, powerful, and amenable to action. As we move into more powerful concepts, the paralysis of excessive analysis will make matters worse, as will deep critiques without equally deep ideas for transcending identified problems. The solution will require us to use complexity and systems theory, but in my use of it, every abstract concept must be accompanied by a practical strategy that illustrates the concept in action. Solutions, in other words, must be theoretical and practical.

This is why I dedicate this book to the new theoreticians—people working on the real problem of transforming real systems, learning by doing it.

I start by discussing eight main elements of an evolving sustainable system, but let's be humble. Addressing the problem of sustainability is the ultimate, adaptive challenge, to use Heifetz's words (Heifetz, 2003; Heifetz & Linsky, 2002):

> An adaptive challenge is a problem for which solutions lie outside the current way of operating. We can distinguish technical problems, which are amenable to current expertise, from adaptive problems, which are not. (Heifetz, 2003, p. 70)

EIGHT ELEMENTS OF SUSTAINABILITY

Sustainability is an adaptive challenge par excellence. As I see it, there are at least eight elements of sustainability:

1. Public service with a moral purpose

2. Commitment to changing context at all levels

3. Lateral capacity building through networks

4. Intelligent accountability and vertical relationships (encompassing both capacity building and accountability)

5. Deep learning

6. Dual commitment to short-term and long-term results

7. Cyclical energizing

8. The long lever of leadership

These eight elements are introduced in this chapter and pursued throughout the book. While I use them in relation to education, these very same strategies can be applied to any public service and to corporate institutions.

1. Public Service With a Moral Purpose

Chapman (2003) talks about the new agenda for public value. Public value, he says, is increased when

- The level of service provision is improved.
- The quality of service is increased.
- The equity or fairness with which service is delivered is increased.
- The service provision is more sustainable and takes into account the needs of future generations.
- The provision of the service is done in a way consistent with the expectations of a liberal diverse society.
- The service provision enhances the level of trust between government and citizens. (p. 128)

Barber (2004) advocates "the enabling state" (in contrast to "the minimalist state") in which strong public services:

- Are universal and diverse
- Respond to the needs and aspiration of citizens
- Compete with the private sector on quality

In Barber's model quality of implementation and short- and long-term outcomes are just as crucial as purpose.

In examining moral purpose (Fullan, 2003b), I talked about how it must transcend the individual to become an organization and system quality in which collectivities are committed to three aspects of moral purpose: (1) raising the bar and closing the gap of student learning; (2) treating people with demanding respect (moral purpose is supportive, responsive, and demanding, depending on the circumstances); and (3) altering the social environment (e.g., other schools and districts) for the better.

Public value and moral purpose have always been the mission statements of democratic governments. This time it is different because the eight elements of sustainability, once pursued in combination, compel all levels of the system to take moral purpose seriously.

2. Commitment to Changing Context at All Levels

David Hargreaves (2003) reminds us of Donald Schon's observation, more than 30 years ago:

We must . . . become adept at learning. We must become able not only to transform our institutions, in response to changing situations and requirements; we must invest and develop institutions which are "learning systems," that is to say, systems capable of bringing about their own continuing transformation. (cited in Hargreaves, p. 74)

It is not Schon's fault that 30 years later, this advice remains 100% accurate but of little practical use. How do you enter the chicken-and-egg equation of starting down the path of generating learning systems in practice, especially in an era of transparent accountability? Again, this book is about providing a practical response to this question; and there is now more powerful (and practical in the high-yield sense) evidence that "changing the system" is an essential component of producing learning organizations.

Put another way, what is it going to take to address Tom Bentley's (2003) challenge?

Recent reform has shown that short-term improvements in key areas such as numeracy and literacy scores, hospital waiting times and street crime are possible. But embedding high expectations and performance permanently in the workings of public service organizations means changing "whole systems," often radically, and equipping them to adapt more effectively to ongoing change. (p. 9)

Changing whole systems means changing the entire context within which people work. Researchers are fond of observing that "context is everything," usually in reference to why a particular innovation succeeded in one situation but not another. Well, if context is everything, we must directly focus on how it can be changed for the better. It is not as impossible as it sounds, although it will take time and cumulative effort. The good news is that once it is under way, it has self-generating powers to go further.

Contexts are the structure and cultures within which one works. In the case of educators, the tri-level contexts are school/community, district, and system. The question is, can we identify strategies that will indeed change in a desirable direction the contexts that affect us? (Currently, these contexts have a neutral or adverse affect on what we do.)

On a small scale, Gladwell (2000) has already identified context as a key "tipping point": "The power of context says that what really matters is the little things" (p. 150). And if you want to change people's behavior, "You need to create a community around them, where these new beliefs could be practical, expressed and nurtured" (p. 173). Drawing from complexity theory, I have already made the case that if you want to change systems, you need to increase the amount of purposeful interaction between and among *individuals* within and across the tri-levels, and indeed within and across *systems* (Fullan, 2003a).

Setting targets and mandatory "annual yearly progress," as is the case with No Child Left Behind, will change only a tiny slice of the context and is neither large enough nor powerful enough to motivate or give people the capacity to succeed. It is also crucial to emphasize that we are not talking about changing the context just for local schools; context change for all levels of the system is essential. New capacity and actions are required at all three levels and in their interactions across levels.

So, we need first of all to commit to pursuing public value through changing context. Then, at a more practical level, each of the remaining six elements soon to be discussed literally gives people new experiences, new capacities, and new insights into what should and can be accomplished. It gives people a taste of the power of new context, none more so than the discovery of lateral capacity building.

3. Lateral Capacity Building Through Networks

I say "discovery" because the sequence was as follows: greater accountability leading to the realization that support or capacity building was essential, which led to vertical capacity building with external trainers at the district or other levels, and then, in turn, to the realization that lateral capacity building across peers was a powerful learning strategy.

In Chapter 5, we will describe lateral capacity across schools, where principals and teacher leaders collaborate with other schools to learn from and contribute to school improvement, not only in individual schools, but also in the district as a whole.

The most systematic strategy-driven use of networks and collaboratives is evolving in England, partly as a response to the limitations of "informed prescription." For example, the government has launched a consultant leaders program in which 1,000 primary school principals who have been successful at improving literacy achievement in their schools are linked (on a 4-to-1 basis) with 4,000 other school principals who want to learn to be more effective in this domain. Thus in this one strategy alone, 20% of all school principals in the country are involved in mutual learning.

Many of the new network strategies in England are being developed by the National College of School Leadership (NCSL). In two publications, NCSL describes "networked learning communities." In *Why Networked Learning Communities*, NCSL (2003b) states

> Collaboration rather than competition is the motivation for hundreds of schools in this pioneering programme that will transform learning experiences for children, teachers and school leaders. (p. 1)

Another project, *Like No Other Initiative* (NCSL, 2003a), states

> The proposition was that schools seeking to become professional learning communities could achieve this more appropriately and more profoundly by working together interdependently in networks. (p. 1)

Since 2002, more than 100 such networks have been funded. All in all, NCSL states that there are six forms of learning promoted in the networks: pupil learning, adult learning, leadership for learning and leadership development, schoolwide learning, school-to-school learning, and network-to-network learning.

In other initiatives, groups of Local Education Authorities (LEAs, or districts) are networked in order to learn from each other about specific topics, such as how to establish efficient and effective "assessing for learning" systems.

There are a number of obvious benefits from lateral strategies (see also D. Hargreaves, 2003, *Education Epidemic*). People learn best from peers (fellow travelers who are further down the road) if there is sufficient opportunity for ongoing, purposeful exchange; the system is designed to foster, develop, and disseminate innovative practices that work—discoveries, let's say, in relation to Heifetz's adaptive challenges ("solutions that lie outside the current way of operating"); leadership is developed and mobilized in many quarters;

and motivation and ownership at the local level are deepened, a key ingredient for sustainability of effort and engagement.

Networks are potentially powerful but can have their downsides. First, there may come to be too many of them, adding clutter instead of focus. Second, they may exchange beliefs and opinions more than quality knowledge, and in any case, what are the processes that could determine the quality and use of knowledge? Third, networks are usually outside the line-authority; so the question is, how do potentially good ideas get out of the networks, so to speak, and into focused implementation, which requires intensity of effort over time in given settings? Networks are not ends in themselves, but must be assessed in terms of their contribution to changing the cultures of schools and districts in the direction of the eight elements of sustainability, including, as we are about to discuss, more effective, less cumbersome accountability schemes.

It is also important to note that lateral capacity is not the only strategy at work (in particular, the relationship to the other seven elements of sustainability must be highlighted). Complexity theory tells us that if you increase the amount of purposeful interaction and infuse it with the checks and balances of quality knowledge, *self-organizing* patterns (desirable outcomes) will accrue. This promise is not good enough for the sustainability-seeking society with a sense of urgency. This is why we need the new theoreticians who are working diligently to establish the eight elements of sustainability.

4. Intelligent Accountability and Vertical Relationships

Sustainable societies must solve (hold in dynamic "tension") the perennial change problem of how to get both local ownership (including capacity) and external accountability, and to get this in the entire system. We know that the problems have to be solved locally:

> Solutions rely, at least in part, on the users themselves and their capacity to take shared responsibility for positive outcomes. In learning, health, work, and even parenting, positive outcomes arise from a combination of personal effort and wider social resources. (Bentley & Wilsdon, 2003, p. 20)

The question is, what is going to motivate people to seek positive outcomes, and when it comes to the public good, how are people and groups to be held accountable? The answer is a mixture of collaboration and networks, on one hand, and what David Miliband, Minister of State for School Standards in Britain, calls "intelligent accountability," on the other hand. Networks and other professional learning communities (lateral capacity building) do build in a strong but not complete measure of accountability. As such communities interact around given problems, they generate better practices, shared commitment, and accountability to peers. As we will see in later chapters, collaborative cultures are demanding when it comes to results, and the demand is telling because it is peer based and up-close on a daily basis.

Vertical relationships (state/district, district/school, etc.) must also be strengthened. One aspect of vertical relationships involves support and resources; the other concerns accountability. Some aspects of accountability will come in the form of Elements 5 (deep learning) and 6 (short-term and long-term results). It will be difficult to get the balance of accountability right in terms of vertical authority: Too much intrusion demotivates people; too little permits drift, or worse.

To address this problem, we need to reintroduce a strategy that has been around for at least 20 years, namely, "self-evaluation," or "school self-review," as it is now called (see Hopkins, 2001; Macbeath, Schratz, Meuret, & Jakobsen, 2000). In the past, self-evaluation has been touted as an alternative to top-down assessment. In fact, we need to conceive of self-evaluation and use it as a both/and solution. New tools for school self-review are now available with the latter goal in mind (several districts in England are now engaged in such development).

Miliband (2004), in a recent speech, put it this way in advocating

An accountability framework, which puts a premium on ensuring effective and ongoing self-evaluation in every school combined with more focused external inspection, linked closely to the improvement cycle of the school. (p. 6)

He then proposes

First, we will work with the profession to create a suite of materials that will help schools evaluate themselves honestly. The balance here is between making the process over-prescriptive, and making it just an occasional one-off event. In the best schools it is continuous, searching and objective. Second, [we] will shortly be making proposals on inspection, which take full account of a school's self-evaluation. A critical test of the strong school will be the quality of its self-evaluation and how it is used to raise standards. Third, the Government and its partners at local and national level will increasingly use the information provided by a school's self-evaluation and development plan, alongside inspection, to inform outcomes about targeting support and challenge. (p. 8)

Despite David Miliband's reference to intelligent accountability, three unions in England just released a paper advocating that "assessment for learning" be reclaimed by the teaching profession. They say, in effect, that the government's intelligent accountability does not rely enough on teacher assessment and judgment.

The union leaders argue that teacher assessment is at the heart of effective learning. The type of assessment that best supports learning is one based on the day-to-day informed professional judgments that teachers make about pupils' learning achievement and their learning needs (Association of Teachers and Lecturers, National Union of Teachers and Professional Association of Teachers, 2004, p. 2).

In other words, the area of accountability and assessment (of and for learning) is going to be contentious no matter how skilled each side becomes at claiming they have the most balanced approach that is best for students and the public. So, it will be very difficult to combine self-evaluation and outside evaluation, but this is the sophistication of sustainability—for the latter to have a chance, *the whole system* must be involved in a codependent partnership, being open to addressing problems as they arise. The new theoreticians on both sides of the accountability issue should be able to come up with a workable approach, acknowledging that it will always be in dynamic tension.

Another critical reason why the whole system must be engaged and why vertical integration must harness horizontal creativity concerns the problem of overload, multiple innovations, and fragmentation or lack of coherence (Fullan, 2001). Education and the public service more broadly do not suffer from too few innovations, but rather from too many ad hoc, unconnected, superficial innovations. Vertical integration is not the only coherence-maker, but it is a key one. The system or organization itself must constantly work on connecting the dots, capturing valuable emerging ideas and patterns. Coherence-making makes complexity simpler. Gathering and paying attention to quality data is learning toward coherence.

5. Deep Learning

Sustainability by our definition requires continuous improvement, adaptation, and collective problem solving in the face of complex challenges that keep arising. As Heifetz (2003) says, adaptive work "demands learning," "demands experimentation," and "difficult conversations." "Species evolve whereas cultures learn," says Heifetz (p. 75).

There are three big requirements for the data-driven society: drive out fear; set up a system of transparent data-gathering coupled with mechanisms for acting on the data; make sure *all* levels of the system are expected to learn from their experiences. Deep learning is for students, teachers, schools, districts, and governments if sustainability is to have any chance.

First, then, is to reduce the fear factor. One of W. E. Deming's (1986) prescriptions for success was "Drive out fear." In the *Education Epidemic,* David Hargreaves (2003) argues

> Government must give active permission to schools to innovate and provide a climate in which failure can be given a different meaning as a necessary element in making progress, as is the case in the business world. . . . Mistakes can be accepted or even encouraged, provided that they are a means of improvement. (p. 36)

Hargreaves quotes

> The fastest way to succeed is to double your failure rate. (Thomas Watson, IBM)
> Fail often to succeed sooner. (Tom Kelley, IDEO)
> You must learn to fail intelligently. Failing is one of the greatest arts in the world. One fails forward towards success. (Thomas Edison) (p. 35)

Or if you like, try the title of Farson and Keyes's (2002) *Whoever Makes the Most Mistakes Wins.*

Hyperbole aside, the point is to not fail stupidly (you are not allowed to keep making the same mistake) but to fail intelligently (forgive and remember). The latter is very much linked to sustainability. Pfeffer and Sutton (2000), in *The Knowing-Doing Gap,* devoted a whole chapter to "When Fear Prevents Acting on Knowledge." In organization after organization, they found that an atmosphere of fear and distrust prevented knowledge from being translated into action (p. 109).

Significantly, Pfeffer and Sutton (2002) identify two other "pernicious effects." One is that "fear causes a focus on the short run [driving] out consideration of the longer run" (pp. 124–125). The other problem is that "fear creates a focus on the individual rather than the collective" (p. 126). In a punitive culture, if I can blame others or others make mistakes, I am better off. Need I say that both the focus on the short run and excessive individualism are fatal for sustainability?

We also see why heavy-handed schemes like No Child Left Behind (NCLB) in the United States and a prescriptive preoccupation with targets in England during the 1990s are bad for sustainability.

Second, capacities and means of acting on the data are critical for learning. Thus "assessment for learning" has become a powerful, high-yield tool for school improvement and student learning (see especially Black, Harrison, Lee, Marshall, & Wiliam, 2003; Hill & Crevola, 2003; Stiggins, 2001). Critical aspects of the move toward more effective data use include (a) avoiding excessive assessment demands (Miliband (2004) talks about reducing necessary paper and information burden, which distract schools from their core business); (b) ensure that a range of data are collected—qualitative as well as quantitative. In *Leading in a Culture of Change* (Chapter 4, "Knowledge Building," Fullan, 2001), I cite several examples, including the U.S. Army's "After Action Reviews," which have three standardized questions: What was supposed to happen? What happened? And what accounts for the differences? This kind of learning is directed to the future, that is, to sustainable improvements.

Third, deep learning is for all levels of the system. At schools and districts, it means collaborative cultures of inquiry that alter the culture of learning in the organization away from dysfunctional and non-relationships toward the daily development of culture that can solve difficult or adaptive problems (see especially Kegan & Lahey, 2001; Perkins, 2003). The 'curriculum" for doing this is contained in Kegan and Lahey's seven languages for transformation (e.g., from the language of complaint to the language of commitment) and in Perkins's developmental leadership, which promotes "progressive interaction" that evokes the exchange of good ideas and fosters the cohesiveness of the group. These new ways of working involve deep changes in the culture of most organizations, and thus the training and development must be sophisticated and intense. Perkins emphasizes how difficult this is going to be. He makes the case that "regressive interaction" (poor knowledge exchange and weak social cohesion) is more likely to occur because it is easier than trying to create the more complex progressive cultures. More about Kegan and Lahey and Perkins later. The point here is that we need a critical mass of new leaders who can move school systems in the direction of deep learning.

And, of course, deep learning for the organization is a necessary condition for fostering deep learning for students of the kind portrayed by Bereiter (2002), Claxton (2002) National Research Council (1999), and others, which includes a greater voice and role for students to shape their own learning and understanding.

Finally, learning from data and experience is not just for schools, but for all levels equally, district and government as well. For example:

> In reality, the system is truly transformed when its central bureaucracy is also transformed, itself becoming an example of the learning organization that it advocates for schools. (D. Hargreaves, 2003, p. 87)

Governments thus would have to rethink their relationships to districts and schools (combining intelligent accountability and lateral-capacity-building strategies, for instance), *and* they would have to develop habits and mechanisms for learning from their actions (internally in the organization and externally). In other words, they need to learn how to constantly adjust, revise, abandon, expand strategies, and so on, according to their efficacy.

6. Dual Commitment to Short-Term and Long-Term Results

Like most aspects of sustainability, things that look as if they are mutually exclusive have to be brought together. It's a pipe dream to argue only for the long-term goal of society, because the public won't let you get away with it, nor should they. The new reality is that governments have to show progress in relation to social priorities (whether it be wait time for health service, street crime, or student achievement) *within one election term* (typically 4 years). Our knowledge base is such that there is no excuse for failing to design and implement strategies that get short-term results.

Of course, short-term progress can be accomplished at the expense of the mid- to long term (win the battle, lose the war), but it doesn't have to be. What I am advocating in this book is that governments and schools set aspirational targets, take action to obtain early results, and intervene in situations of terrible performance, all the while investing in the eight sustainability capacity-building elements described in this chapter. Over time, the system gets stronger, and fewer severe problems occur as they are preempted by corrective action sooner rather than later (see also Chapter 7).

Short-term results are also necessary to build trust with the public for longer-term investments. Michael Barber (2004) argues that it is necessary to

> Create the virtuous circle where public education delivers results, the public gains confidence and is therefore willing to invest through taxation and, as a consequence, the system is able to improve further. It is for this reason that the long-term strategy requires short-term results. (p. 2)

This is the time to say that sustainability is resource hungry but in such a way that conserves, refocuses, and reduces waste, as well as results in *growing financial investment* over time (Barber & Fullan, 2004). It is a paradox that sustainability both produces and consumes more resources—none more valuable than individual and collective energy.

7. Cyclical Energizing

Sustain comes from the Latin word *sustineo,* which means "to keep up," but this is misleading. Sustainability, on the contrary, is not linear. It is cyclical, for two fundamental reasons. One has to do with energy, and the other with periodic plateaus, where additional time and ingenuity are required for the next adaptive breakthrough. Loehr and Schwartz's (2003) "power of full engagement" argues that "energy, not time" is the fundamental currency of high performance. They base their work on four principles:

> Principle 1: Full engagement requires four separate but related sources of energy: physical, emotional, mental, and spiritual. (p. 9)

> Principle 2: Because energy capacity diminishes both with overuse and with underuse, we must balance energy expenditure with intermittent energy renewal. (p. 11)

> Principle 3: To build capacity, we must push beyond our normal limits, training in the same systematic way that elite athletes do. (p. 13)

> Principle 4: Positive energy rituals—highly specific routines for managing energy—are key to full engagement and sustained high performance. (p. 14)

Loehr and Schwartz (2003) are talking about individuals, whereas we are interested as well in systems, but the same logic applies. They contrast the old paradigm with the new:

Manage time versus manage energy.

Avoid stress versus seek stress.

Life is a marathon versus life is a series of sprints.

Downtime is wasted versus downtime is productive time.

Rewards fuel performance versus purpose fuels performance. (p. 6)

If we want sustainability, we need to keep an eye on energy levels (overuse and underuse). Positive collaborative cultures will help because (a) they push for greater accomplishments, and (b) they avoid the debilitating effects of negative cultures. It is not hard work that tires us out as much as it is negative work. But collaborative cultures can become too intense and burn us out. What we need are combinations of full engagement with colleagues, along with less intensive activities that are associated with replenishment.

There is another reason why sustainability is cyclical. In many cases, for reasons stated earlier, we have seen achievement in literacy and mathematics improve over a 5-year period, only to have it plateau or level off. It may be related to burnout, but this is not likely the main explanation. People are still putting in a lot of energy to maintain the same higher-level performance represented by the new plateau. If people were burning out, performance would likely *decline.*

A more likely explanation is that the set of strategies that brought initial success are not the ones—not powerful enough—to take us to higher levels. In these cases, we would expect the best learning organizations to investigate, learn, experiment, and develop better solutions. *This takes time.* (Incidentally, with the right kind of intelligent accountability, we would know whether organizations were engaged in quality problem-solving processes even if their short-term outcomes were not showing increases.)

While this new adaptive work is going on, we would not expect achievement scores to rise in a linear fashion, and any external assessment scheme that demanded "annual yearly progress" would be barking up the wrong tree.

Cyclical energizing is a powerful new idea. We don't yet have the precision to know what cyclical energizing looks like in detail, but the concept needs to be a fundamental element of our sustainability strategizing.

8. The Long Lever of Leadership

Archimedes said, "Give me a lever long enough and I can change the world." For sustainability, that lever is leadership—a certain kind of new leadership described in Chapters 4 through 7—leadership that operates very differently than is the case in the present, that is valued differently by societies seeking greater sustainability, and that helps produce other similar leaders to create a critical mass. This critical mass is the long lever of leadership. If a system is to be mobilized in the direction of sustainability, leadership at all levels must be the primary engine. The main work of these leaders is to help put into place the eight elements of sustainability; all eight simultaneously feeding on each other. To do this, we need a system laced with leaders who are trained to think in bigger terms and to act in ways that affect larger parts of the system as a whole: the new theoreticians.

CHAPTER THREE

Leadership to the Fore

As society places higher and higher expectations on the performance of public and private agencies, leadership is bound to come to the fore. The question is, what kind of leadership is needed for sustainability? In a nutshell, we need a critical mass of leaders at all levels of the system who are explicitly cognizant of and committed to pursuing in practice the implementation of the eight elements of sustainability described in Chapter 2. Systems change on an ongoing basis only if you have enough leaders who are system thinkers. This is what is meant by "thinking outside the box." If you think context, you change context. Let's be very careful here: You can't think precisely enough about context unless you are also *acting* in this enlarged arena. When great thinking and action go hand in hand, the concepts get larger and they also get more meaningful because they are grounded in concrete strategies and actions.

Almost 20 years ago, Peter Block (1987) argued that "cultures get changed in a thousand small ways, not by dramatic announcements emanating from the boardroom" (p. 98). Not fully true. It requires the thousand small ways *and* boardroom policies. Sustainability is a team sport, and the team is large.

In this chapter, I take up where we are now and set the stage for what individuals can do and what systems can do to bring the right kind of leadership to the fore. Subsequent chapters zero in on the new work of leaders as it plays out at the school, district, and system levels.

WHERE WE ARE

Almost everyone agrees that leadership is the key to reform. And then they make mistakes. The most egregious error is the search for the super leader. The title of Khurana's (2002) study of 850 CEOs captures the problem: *Searching for a Corporate Savior: The Irrational Quest for Charismatic CEOs*. As he puts it:

> Perhaps the most fundamental—and fundamentally irrational—attitude underlying the closed CEO market is the belief in charismatic authority itself. The attraction of charismatic leaders is that they promise a solution to all of our problems if only we follow the leaders with unwavering certitude. . . .
>
> For all its manifest defects, charismatic authority has always been alluring for the single reason that it avoids accountability and responsibility for outcomes. (pp. 207–208)

Ironically, the poorer the performance of the company (or school district), the more likely boards will make the fundamental mistake of hiring high-profile CEOs, virtually guaranteeing that continuous improvement over time will not happen:

> When a company performs badly, institutional investors [the public, school board] are likely to demand that the CEO resign and be replaced by someone who is from outside the firm. The external CEO search process that ensues is characterized by unusual secrecy; anxious attention to the expectations of outsiders . . . ; a focus on an extremely small number of candidates, people who are already high-profile leaders; and an emphasis on the elusive, culturally-based qualities of "leadership" and "charisma" at the expense of concrete knowledge of a firm and its problems. (Khurana, 2002, p. xii)

Similarly, Collins (2001) found that charismatic leaders are negatively associated with sustainability. He distinguishes between Level 5 leaders "who build enduring greatness" and Level 4 leaders who "catalyze commitment to a vision and to standards" (p. 20). As Collins laments,

> One of the most damaging trends in recent history is the tendency (especially by boards of directors) to select dazzling,

celebrity leaders and to de-select potential Level 5 leaders [who appear less flashy]. (p. 39)

We don't have comparable in-depth studies of superintendents and principals, but the carousel of superintendent turnover certainly reflects the ad hoc search for the leader who will finally right the ship (see Andy Hargreaves, 2004). David Hargreaves (2003), taking up Collins's (2001) findings, makes a similar point:

When English headteachers are being appointed, they are expected by the governing body to articulate a clear vision for the school, which they promise they will implement if appointed.

Significantly, very few Level 5 leaders were appointed from within the company, whereas among school headteachers, it is more common to appoint from outside than inside. We may have it wrong in education in assuming that "fresh blood at the top" is a lever of school improvement. While this may apply to schools that are (close to) failing, it may need an insider to take a good school to greatness because it builds on what they inherit rather than striving towards a different vision against the inclinations and preferences of the staff. An insider may have a better grasp of the school's weaknesses and is thus able to face the facts brutally and so do something about them. (p. 42)

Sustainability is very much linked to continuity of deepening direction over time. We can describe Collins's Level 5 leaders in these terms: The main mark of an effective principal is not just his or her impact on the bottom line of student achievement, but also on *how many leaders he or she leaves behind who can go even further.* These are not mutually exclusive. Level 5 leaders have a dual focus on performance and development of leadership in others.

There are, however, very few Level 5 leaders (in any sector), which means that there are too few leaders available who are working on developing leaders beyond themselves. In cases of high turnover, such as in education, this is a disastrous situation. Stated differently, it is not turnover per se that is the problem, but rather *discontinuity of direction.*

We can also consider the issue of sustainability from a different angle and ask about "succession." Studies of succession in the principalship are rare, with Andy Hargreaves, Moore, Fink, Brayman, and White's (2003) recent study being an exception. In a review of literature, and in case studies of succession in six high schools, Hargreaves et al. (Hargreaves & Fink, in press) drew disturbing conclusions:

> Four sets of findings emerged from the study. First, succession can bring about *planned continuity* in a school's development where it is doing well, *planned discontinuity* where a school has been underperforming or resting on its laurels, and *unplanned continuity* or *discontinuity* where little thought has gone into the succession process at all. *Planned continuity* was a rare phenomenon and mainly occurred when successful schools groomed insiders to continue the work of the existing principal. *Planned discontinuity* temporarily turned underachieving schools around, but principals were rotated out of their schools too soon, before their work was done, and the schools quickly regressed. In these and other cases, many cases of succession were ones of *unplanned discontinuity* with the prior principal's achievements, and *unplanned continuity* with the mediocrity that preceded them. (Hargreaves et al., 2003, Executive Summary, pp. 1–2; emphasis in original)

In short, there is not much planned continuity going on at all, and when there is, it is short term or weak. There is nothing to inspire us that many Level 4, let alone Level 5, leaders will be spawned. As Andy Hargreaves et al. (2003) conclude

> Sustainable leadership maintains improvement from one leader to the next and spreads across many leaders and schools in a district, not just one or two. What our evidence suggests instead is that principal succession today is not an episodic crisis but a chronic process. Its suddenness and frequency short-circuit most improvement efforts, and its predictable regularity creates longer-term staff cynicism about any and all attempts at change. (p. 80)

The consequences of the failure to focus on succession are amplified under circumstances of high turnover. In every jurisdiction, the current decade represents a massive exodus from the principalship. Williams (2001) found that more than 80% of current elementary and secondary principals in Ontario, Canada, will retire by 2009 (two thirds by 2006). In the United States, it is estimated that 40% of current principals will retire in the next 6 years (Wallace Foundation, 2003). In England, 45% of headteachers and deputies are over 50 years of age, which means there will be a large exodus over the next 10 years (Hartle & Thomas, 2003). In New South Wales, Australia, the mean age of current school principals is just over 50 (Scott, 2003). And so it goes.

It is not so much that there is a shortage of certified principals to fill the vacancies, but rather a shortage of principals with the qualities to help develop the sustainability transformation we are talking about in this book. In the United States, Roza (2003) found that there is not a dearth of certified candidates for the principalship, but rather, two other fundamental issues. First, was a problem of distribution:

Some districts and schools are avoided by prospective principals. Districts and schools with the fewest applicants are typically those with the most challenging working conditions, higher concentrations of poor and minority students, and lower salaries for principals. (p. 7)

A second and equally troubling problem concerns the leadership qualities (as distinct from technical eligibility) of prospective principals:

A serious gap exists between what superintendents say they want in new principals and the experiences human resource departments rely on to screen candidates. . . .
    Superintendents are more interested in the leadership experience and talent of prospective principals than in candidates' administrative or management skill. (Roza, 2003, p. 9)

Regardless of who does the hiring, are there enough candidates with the *leadership* qualities that will be required to take us into new levels? The answer, given the analysis in the previous pages, has to be "no."

Given the dearth of Level 5 leaders, there are two basic problems. First, there are scores of teachers who are working under difficulty; that is, since high-quality leaders help make working conditions energizing and make school improvement exciting, principals who do not possess these qualities do not improve the working lives of teachers.

Second, we can't gain on the problem, because it takes Level 5 leaders to produce more Level 5 leaders. We need to cultivate leaders who can combine Level 4 leadership (catalyzes commitment to visions and standards) and Level 5 leadership (builds enduring greatness). Amalgams of Level 4 and 5 leadership can lead, mentor, and reproduce a critical mass of new leaders who can turn the tide toward powerful new forces for sustainable reform.

Reports from the Office for Standards in Education (OFSTED, 2003b, 2003c) in England found that leadership at the school level had improved over the past 7 years but that there were still many schools where work was not managed effectively. Of course, we are talking about even greater expectations—not management, but leadership that promotes the conditions of sustainability.

Finally, if we ask the question, aren't we demanding too much of the principalship by expecting sustainable leadership? The answer is "yes" *under the current system*. This does not have to remain the case in the future. I reckon it takes about 10 years of cumulative development to become a highly effective school leader. If such development occurs, the job becomes more doable and more exciting because of what can be accomplished. We know, for example, that experts expend less energy in dealing with complex matters because they more easily and subconsciously recognize patterns and intuit effective responses (Ackerman, Pipek, & Wulf, 2003). They become more efficient and more effective because of their (reflective, developmental) experiences. If we then can multiply the opportunities for would-be and practicing principals to obtain new learning experiences—through, for example, strategies described in this book—we enable more and more leaders to develop accordingly. And the more that leaders develop in this direction, the more similar leaders they, in turn, produce. Once these developments reach a critical mass, *the context changes.* As this happens, less energy will be required to yield positive results, with self-generating or sustainable reform becoming possible.

To recap:

1. Leadership is to this decade what standards-based reform was to the 1990s.

2. The main mark of an effective leader at the end of his or her tenure is not so much the impact on the bottom line (of profits or student achievement), but rather how many good leaders he or she leaves behind who can go even further.

3. It is not turnover of leaders, per se, that is the problem, but rather discontinuity of direction.

4. While almost everyone agrees that leadership is key to success, there is insufficient clarity about what the role should be and to what short- and long-term ends.

5. The current "system" is random at best and dysfunctional at worst; put harshly, the current system is guaranteed to produce disruptive leadership rather than to generate cumulative continuity necessary for going deeper over time, which is essential for sustainability.

WHAT INDIVIDUALS CAN DO

Individual sustainability concerns the ability to keep on going without burning out. The key to doing this is not an all-out marathon, but rather cyclical energizing. To do this, leaders need to seek sources and situations that push the limits of their energy and engagement, coupled with rituals or periodic breaks that are energy recovering.

We saw earlier Loehr and Schwartz's (2003) argument for *The Power of Full Engagement*. Leaders have a double reason to address cyclical energizing, because not only does this affect them, but it also has far-reaching consequences for those with whom they work:

Leaders are the stewards of organizational energy. . . . They inspire or demoralize others first by how effectively they manage their own energy and next by how well they mobilize, focus, invest and renew the collective energy of those they lead. (p. 5)

Loehr and Schwartz (2003) make the point that we need to seek and harness four sources of energy—the physical, emotional, mental, and spiritual. But instead of urging leaders to maximize energy, they call for cycles of high performance and recovery:

We grow at all levels by expending energy beyond our ordinary limits and then recovering. Expose a muscle to ordinary demand and it won't grow. With age it will actually lose strength. The limiting factor in building any "muscle" is that many of us back off at the slightest hint of discomfort. To meet increased demand in our lives, we must learn to systematically build and strengthen muscles wherever our capacity is insufficient. Any form of stress that prompts discomfort has the potential to expand our capacity—physically, mentally, emotionally or spiritually—so long as it is followed by adequate recovery. (p. 13)

On "the use it or lose it" dimension, we do need to revisit and stretch our moral purpose: Why did I become a leader in the first place? What do I do to develop and support leaders? How can I share outside my school in order to help other schools develop? In short, fuel and be fueled by our emotional and spiritual sources of energy.

With respect to mental or cognitive energy, work with others to tackle the adaptive challenges we are talking about in this book (see Chapters 5 through 7). Accessing ideas and mobilizing collective energy to address a complex problem can be exciting and satisfying as you grapple with an important matter that has yet to be solved. Work on your emotional intelligence: Emotionally intelligent leaders live longer and more effectively in complex times.

The cluster of energy sources just discussed is very close to one of the eight guidelines in my *Change Forces With a Vengeance* (Fullan, 2003a): "Mobilize the social attractors—moral purpose, quality of relationships and quality knowledge" (p. 24). In short, there are a small number of powerful, positive sources of energy that we can seek out and immerse ourselves in.

There are things you should not do. If you are in a toxic or distrustful culture, you can get ahead by outwitting others, looking after number one, or hoping others will fail. As Peter Block (1987) said, "Why get better at a bad game?" (p. 9). It is not just morally wrong. Let's consider energy. There is actually no shortage of energy in a negative culture. When people are out to get each other, they don't complain about lack of time. Negative actions are amazingly energizing (think *rage*): Aside from their short-term damage, negative actions deenergize us over time. Indeed, negative energy can lead to illness and early death. It is positive energy fully exploited that is related to longevity and hence greater sustainability.

A second recipe for burnout in yourself and those with whom you work is what Goleman, Boyatzis, and McKee (2002) call the "pacesetting" leader. Pacesetters are leaders who expect excellence and exemplify it, who push people to the limit, and who are constantly searching for new ideas. Not bad for short-term performance, but fatal for sustainability:

> Our data show that ... pacesetting poisons the climate—particularly because of the emotional costs when a leader relies on it too much. Essentially, the pacesetter's dilemma is this: The more pressure put on people for results, the more anxiety it provokes. Although moderate pressure can energize people—the challenge of meeting a deadline, for instance—continuous pressure can be debilitating. . . . Although pacesetters may get compliance—and therefore a short-term, upward blip in results—they don't get true performance that people will sustain. (p. 73)

The argument, then, is that the skillful and balanced management of energy is the key to sustainability. Overuse is burnout; underuse is atrophy. Tim Brighouse, the former Director of the Birmingham Education Authority, in England, and now the "Czar" of transforming the London education system, divides the world into energy creators, energy neutrals, and energy consumers (Brighouse & Woods, 1999). He summarizes their characteristics:

Energy creators

- Are enthusiastic and always positive
- Use critical thinking, creativity, and imagination
- Stimulate and spark others
- Practice leadership at all levels
- Are able and willing to scrutinize their practice and willing to make their practice accessible to others
- Wish to improve on their previous best

Energy neutrals are

- Competent, sound practitioners
- Willing to [address] the task
- Good at "maintenance"

- Sometimes uncomfortable accepting examination of their practice by others
- Capable of improving on their previous best

Energy consumers . . . tend to

- Have a negative view of the world
- Resent change and practice blocking strategies
- Use other people's time excessively
- Not feel good about themselves
- Be unable and unwilling to critically examine their teaching practice
- Appear not to want to improve on their personal best. (p. 84)

The goal of would-be individual leaders, of course, is to become more and more like "energy creators" and especially to be aware of how they can cultivate energy creation in other leaders they are in a position to mentor. We know the sources of energy creation: moral purpose, emotional intelligence, quality relationships, quality knowledge, physical well-being—all mobilized to engage the mind and heart in attempting to solve complex adaptive challenges.

There is less acknowledgment in the change literature of *energy recovery*. Virtually all the positive press on leadership is about developing and energizing people, and little on strategies of recovery. Because of this neglect, even the most motivated leaders will not last and will not leave lasting legacies.

I provide here some initial ideas about energy recovery, but the broader call is that the massive attention currently being paid to leadership needs to include a conceptual and strategic focus on cycles of energy renewal.

It seems to me that there are two types of energy-recovery strategies: One is built into daily or weekly routines, which we could call "rituals" (after Loehr & Schwartz, 2003); the other is more cyclical, which I will refer to as "periodic."

Loehr and Schwartz (2003) refer to "positive energy rituals," which are highly specific routines for managing energy:

The sustaining power of rituals comes from the fact that they conserve energy. . . . In contrast to will and discipline, which imply pushing ourselves to action, a well-defined ritual pulls us. We feel somehow worse if we don't do it. Think about brushing your teeth or taking a shower or kissing your spouse goodbye in the morning. . . . If we want to build into our lives new behaviors that last, we can't spend much energy to sustain them. (p. 169)

And:

The power of rituals is that they insure that we use as little conscious energy as possible where it is not absolutely necessary, leaving us free to strategically focus the energy available to us in creative, enriching ways.

Look at any part of your life in which you are consistently effective and you will find that certain habits make that possible. If you eat in a healthy way, it is probably because you have built routines around the food you buy and what you are willing to order at restaurants. . . . If you are successful in a sales job, you probably have a ritual of mental preparation for calls and ways that you talk to yourself to stay positive in the face of rejection. . . . If you sustain high energy despite an extremely demanding job, you almost certainly have predictable ways of insuring that you get intermittent recovery. Creating positive rituals is the most powerful means we have found to effectively manage energy in the service of full engagement. (pp. 14–15)

Eating habits, physical fitness, meditation, reflective journal writing, and taking short time-outs all qualify as positive rituals. Leaders who are to be effective over the long haul will need to establish their own combinations of rituals.

Periodic recovery consists of cycles of activity that take place over longer periods of time. Since all effective leaders are immersed in daily relationships, getting away from the group now and then can be a great source of personal renewal. The psychologist Anthony Storr (1988) shows how solitude can be a source of personal meaning and creativity:

The capacity to be alone is a valuable resource when changes of mental attitude are required. . . . In a culture in which interpersonal relationships are generally considered to provide the answer to every form of distress, it is sometimes difficult to persuade well-meaning helpers that solitude can be as therapeutic as emotional support. (p. 29)

Solitude, says Storr (1988), facilitates "learning, thinking, innovation, and maintaining contact with one's own inner world" (p. 29).

As we contemplate promoting and balancing full engagement with renewal, we come to the intersection of the individual and the system. If the system is relentlessly demanding, or for that matter, if it is casually permissive, it is not possible to become or stay productively engaged. In one study, Flintham (2003) talks about "when reservoirs run dry" in referring to why principals leave the headship. These school leaders "had key messages regarding the value of . . . professional development reinforced by strategic reflection opportunities and an infrastructure of peer support to reinforce this" (p. 3).

We are about to turn to the system side of the equation, but the message for the individual leader is to push the system by "Getting better at a good game." Look for ways to cultivate other leaders as you focus on performance; participate in networks and other knowledge-sharing opportunities as these involve. I won't go so far as to say that if enough individuals get good at this new game that sustainability will replace survival in leadership, but we won't get any breakthroughs in the absence of individuals doing their part.

In addition to individual effort, we need, as I have argued, a more direct and explicit focus on changing *systems*.

WHAT SYSTEMS CAN DO

Systems consist of individuals, so what does it mean to say that systems must change, and, furthermore, that they must change toward sustainability? My answer is that you do this through leaders at the system level and all other levels, becoming *explicitly conscious* that they are engaged in widening people's experiences and identification beyond their normal bailiwicks. The proposition is that the key to changing systems is to produce greater numbers of "system thinkers." If more and more leaders become system thinkers, they will gravitate toward strategies that alter people's system-related experiences; that is, they will alter people's mental awareness of the system as a whole, thereby contributing to altering the system itself.

I do not think we have made any progress at all in actually promoting systems thinking since Peter Senge (1990) first raised the matter. Let's consider Senge's first description:

> Human endeavors are also systems. They . . . are bound by invisible fabrics of interrelated actions, which often take years to fully play out their effects on each other. Since we are part of the lacework work ourselves, it is doubly hard to see the whole pattern of change. Instead, we tend to focus on snapshots of isolated parts of the system, and wonder why our deepest problems never seem to get solved. Systems thinking is a conceptual framework, a body of knowledge and tools that has been developed over the past fifty years, to make the full patterns clearer, and *to help us see how to change them effectively.* (p. 7; my emphasis)

We will come back to the italics later, but most of us will recall that systems thinking is the fifth discipline, which integrates the other four disciplines: personal mastery, mental models, building shared vision, and team learning.

Philosophically, Senge (1990) is on the right track, but it doesn't seem to be very helpful in practice:

> [Systems thinking] is the discipline that integrates the disciplines, fusing them into a coherent body of theory and practice. It keeps them from being separate gimmicks or the latest organization fads. Without a systemic orientation, there is no motivation to look at how the disciplines interrelate. . . .
>
> At the heart of a learning organization is a shift of mind—from seeing ourselves as separate from the world to connected to the world, from seeing problems as caused by someone or something "out there" to seeing how our own actions create the problems we experience. A learning organization is a place where people are continually discovering how they create their reality *and how they can change it.* (pp. 12, 13; my emphasis)

With at least a decade of work, I don't think we have made any significant gains on defining the problem, let alone doing anything about it. The fifth discipline "fieldbook" takes up the issue of application (Senge et al., 2000). We see once again that "the discipline of systems thinking provides a different way of looking at problems and goals—not as isolated events but as components of larger structures" (p. 78). There is then a discussion of how the term *systems thinking* has been used in a confusing manner, with the new suggestion that there is actually a continuum of seven approaches: "system-wide thinking," "open systems thinking," "human systems thinking," "process systems thinking," "living systems thinking," and "feedback-simulation" (Senge et al., 2000, p. 79).

This doesn't seem to be a "continuum," and more important from the perspective of the new theoretician seeking system impact, there is nothing practical to go on. If anything, the situation seems more confusing.

In the fifth discipline fieldbook, systems thinking is applied to staff development:

> All too often there is little communication across grade levels and across content areas. A child gets an experience in one year that might not relate to the next year's experience. This situation makes the school particularly vulnerable to tests, because each year's instructor feels that he or she alone must prepare the kids for assessment. But aligning curriculum across levels requires using the skills and technologies of systems thinking and mental models; you have to get agreement among all the teachers about where the starting level for students exists and how fast to carry them along the development path. . . .
>
> If you're a systems thinker in school planning, then you focus not on particular practices but on building collaborative relationships and structures for change. You need mechanisms and a process that allow people to talk, across grade levels, departments, and schools within a system. (Senge et al., 2000, p. 394)

It is not so much a criticism of Senge's (1990) work as it is a commentary on the field of system thinking to note that we are not making any progress at fostering it in practice. Here is my take:

1. Yes, we know that current systems are working in isolation with terrible results, but we have known that for years.

2. Yes, collaboration is key, and "you have to get agreement among all the teachers," but how do you do that, not to mention agreement among districts, governments, and the public?

3. Systems thinking is not just a cognitive endeavor in order to discover the whole picture and long-term trends. As my italics from Senge's quote emphasize, the goal is to understand the system and change it for the better.

4. Systems thinking means not only that given individuals or organizations can appreciate and take into account the larger system but also that individuals and organizations can be engaged with others outside themselves in order to change the very system that surrounds them.

5. For systems thinking to have its intended affect, it can't be for a small group of specialists; it must be made practically accessible to the large group of new and emerging leaders.

Earlier, I said we need powerful concepts of change but that the power will be realized only if the concepts can be rendered understandable by typical intelligent leaders, not by a subgroup specializing in the topic. I said that for every abstract concept, we need to be able to point to a corresponding concrete policy or strategy that is intended to advance the concept in practice.

Thus, one core goal of this book is to identify ideas and strategies that will promote systems thinking. Systems thinking in practice, in turn, is the key to sustainability. On the practice side, I maintain that it is possible and necessary to give leaders experiences that increase their ability to take the larger picture into account. When leaders get such experience, they obtain an increment in systems thinking, and when the latter happens, they are more included to share and to identify with others in pursuit of larger, more meaningful system goals. When this happens, systems themselves change for the better.

We need to be clear. I am not talking about producing armchair system thinkers. It will be "system thinkers in action" who count. They may not have the best elaborate theories of how systems evolve over the long run, but they will be in the midst of action with a system perspective. And they will interact with others to promote system awareness through their actions and conversations, as we demonstrate in upcoming chapters.

As we focus on system sustainability, one critical aspect to address is what cyclical energizing means at the organization and system levels. Just as individuals have to enter cycles of push and recovery, so do systems. What this means has not been addressed in the literature. It will include not aggravating the overload problem by piling policies upon policies, working on alignment so that the deenergizing effects of fragmentation do not take their toll, taking time out to review and consolidate gains, celebrating accomplishments, investing more resources as success accrues, and, of course, fostering the development of leadership at all levels of the organization and system.

More generally, I have suggested eight correlated strategies for sustainability (Chapter 2). Elements of these strategies are already in place in some jurisdictions. Networks and collaboratives, for example, can increase leaders' capacities to see wider and farther, provided that they also contribute to leaders' clarity and coherence of system purpose and dynamics. Leaders at the system level need to engage other levels so that policies and strategies are shaped and reshaped, and the emerging bigger picture is constantly communicated and critiqued. They need to give other leaders within the system many experiences to widen their interaction and knowledge base and to question central direction. Local leaders for their part must push outward to lead lateral capacity building and vertical exchanges with higher levels of the system as a whole.

In short, in a would-be sustainable world, "leadership to the fore" means the proliferation of systems thinkers in action.

CHAPTER FOUR

The New Work of Leaders

In essence, the new work entails leaders immersing themselves in the eight elements of sustainability. We have just seen some of the general implications of this work at the individual and system levels. In this chapter, I probe more deeply into the nature of this work. In subsequent chapters (5, 6, 7), I apply the ideas to the work of leaders at the school/community, district, and system levels.

We talked earlier about Heifetz and Linsky's (2002) critically important distinction between technical and adaptive solutions. Technical solutions involve solving problems that can be addressed through current knowledge or know-how; adaptive challenges concern problems whose solutions are not known. Moving literacy achievement scores up to 75% for 11-year-olds, as they did in England, is a technical solution; going beyond this plateau is an adaptive challenge. Of course, working on the eight components of sustainability in Chapter 2 is an adaptive challenge of the highest order.

The portal to this new arena of learning can be found readily by considering four of Heifetz's (2004) properties of an adaptive challenge:

1. The challenge consists of a gap between aspiration and reality, demanding a response outside our current repertoire.

2. Adaptive work to narrow the gap requires difficult learning.

3. The people with the problem are the problem, and they are the solution.

4. Adaptive work generates disequilibrium and avoidance.

In other words, addressing an adaptive challenge requires complex learning in politically contentious situations where there are many inertial forces pulling us back to the status quo (or, if you like, keeping us from persisting in addressing the challenge). While this may seem impossible work, there are ideas, strategies, and ways of approaching adaptive challenges that are specific and practical, albeit requiring a critical mass of sophisticated leaders.

My entry point for these strategies is Element 5 on sustainability—deep learning—problem solving applied to all. In Chapter 2, I introduced Perkins's (2003) *King Arthur's Roundtable* and Kegan and Lahey's (2001) *How the Way We Talk Can Change the Way We Work*. Now, I take up the argument in more detail as it so powerfully maps onto our agenda. (The following quotations in this chapter are from these two sources.)

Perkins's (2003) basic question is, "What is organizational intelligence, why is it so hard to come by, and how can we get more of it" (p. 14)? To which his general reply is:

> How smart an organization or community is reflects the kinds of conversations that people have with one another, taking conversations in a broad sense to include all sorts of interactions. (p. 14)

Perkins makes the distinction between progressive interactions that move the organization forward and regressive interactions that slow things down or make them worse. He talks about interactions that are "process smart" and "people smart," or their opposites:

> *Process smart* means that progressive interactions exchange information and ideas in ways that foster astute decisions, good solutions and far-seeing plans. *People smart* means that progressive interactions foster the cohesiveness of the group, leaving people feeling good about working together and looking forward to doing more together . . . [acknowledging] that a certain amount of conflict is productive. . . . As to process, regressive interactions exchange information and ideas in narrow, confused and cautious ways. Key information gets lost. Plans are less informed than they might be; decisions are lopsided. As to people, regressive interactions constitute a kind of centrifugal force, pushing people apart through dissatisfactions, rivalries, and lack of vision more than they pull people together. (pp. 20–21; his emphasis)

Process smart means good knowledge on an ongoing basis; people smart means emotional identity with the group and its values.

> Progressive interactions involve effective knowledge processing and positive symbolic conduct, the kind of symbolic conduct that builds cohesiveness, trust, and commitment. (Perkins, 2003, p. 29)

What is the difficulty? Why not just expand the frequency of progressive interactions? Regressive archetypes are cognitively and emotionally simpler and easier to use; progressive practices require much more skill and persistence. Moreover, conditions and human nature in complex times favor regressive actions:

> In times of stress, when cognitive load is high, behavior tends to regress toward simpler earlier-learned behaviors. And it's hard to be progressive when the other guy is being regressive. Both progressive and regressive practices stimulate their own kind, but regressive practices tend to provoke regressive practices more than progressive practices provoke progressive practices. (Perkins, 2003, p. 247)

We will return to Perkins in a moment, but let's first reintroduce another compatible set of lenses and tools, namely, Kegan and Lahey's (2001) power of certain kinds of conversation. It's the same adaptive problem that Heifetz (2003) and Perkins make us confront.

Leading inevitably involves trying to effect significant changes.

- It is very hard to bring about significant changes in any human group without changes in individual behaviors.
- It is very hard to *sustain* significant changes in behavior without significant changes in individuals' underlying meanings that may give rise to their behaviors.
- It is very hard to lead on behalf of other people's changes in their underlying ways of making meaning without considering the possibility that we ourselves must also change. (Kegan & Lahey, 2001, p. 3; emphasis in original)

Kegan and Lahey (2001) then present seven "languages of transformation," with practical methodology for how to use them:

1. From the language of complaint to the language of commitment.

2. From the language of blame to the language of personal responsibility.

3. From the language of "New Year's Resolutions" to the language of competing commitments.

4. From the language of big assumptions that hold us to the language of assumptions that we hold . . .

5. From the language of prizes and praising to the language of ongoing regard.

6. From the language of rules and policies to the language of public agreement.

7. From the language of constructive criticism to the language of deconstructive criticism. (pp. 8–9)

Easier said than done, as Kegan and Lahey (2001) take us through some of the hidden assumptions that keep us from moving to the right half of the above equations. They do provide a methodology for moving toward the new languages, which also demonstrates how difficult it will be to do so. Yet the point is that the new languages are essential for sustainability; and they are *doable* in the sense that you can get better at them through reflective practice.

There are two remaining critical points. One is to nail down what we are *not* talking about; the other is to identify the key lever for transformation.

On the former matter, let's be crystal clear that this is not about increasing the sheer amount of conversation and talk in the organization. Perkins (2003) calls this "coblaboration":

The dark side of collaboration deserves a name of its own. Let's call it *coblaboration*. The aim is to collaborate, but the result is blab that does not really pool the minds around the table, going nowhere in any one of several different ways, or all of them. (p. 149; emphasis in original)

Of course, the left half of Kegan and Lahey's (2001) seven languages are all examples of how talk can be cheap, negative, useless, damaging—languages of complaint, blame, meaningless (New Year's) resolutions, unquestioning assumptions, superficial prizes and praising, rules and policies, and constructive (but ineffective) criticism. Add to this three faces of dysfunctional "blab"—"Brownian motion" (random discussion that drifts); "downward spiraling" (conversations get stuck); and "groupthink" (people thinking too much alike or agreeing too readily).

> Brownian motion has people jumping around too much, and downspiraling has them stuck in a hole, but groupthink catches them settling too easily into comfortable conclusions. (Perkins, 2003, p. 152)

Progressive interactions and the languages of transformation find value in certain kinds of conflict and deal with it productively; provide feedback that is conducive to learning; access good knowledge on an ongoing basis; make people feel committed; generate patterns of cumulative coherence; help people focus collectively; are reflective-action oriented (strong on doing); and give people experiences outside themselves that foster system thinkers in action.

What is it going to take to change the languages of organizations? Once again, the answer is a critical mass of new leaders. In the language of this chapter, Kegan and Lahey (2001) say that we need leaders who are effective at "leading the language community":

> The idea is not only that leaders should pay attention to how they speak and what they say but also that leaders have the opportunity to create places or channels for . . . forms of communication between and among all the members of the community. (p. 188)

Perkins (2003) goes further:

> Progressive interactions build organizational intelligence and encourage people to step in that direction by giving communicative feedback, exercising inquiry-centered leadership, avoiding coblaboration, and cultivating trust in a common vision and civil process. (p. 210)

As we get closer to action, Perkins (2003) makes the critical distinction between "explanation theories" and "action theories."

Explanation theories explain things such as what is wrong and why, but provide no direction for what to do about the situation. Action theories are directed at how to accomplish things. The problem is the latter theories are not very sophisticated or helpful. They may tell us what to do, but are often explanation theories disguised as action theories; that is, you might read the action theory and still not know what to do or how to do it.

Instead, Perkins (2003) calls for "action poetry":

> The language of real change needs not just explanation theories, or even action theories, but good action poetry—action theories that are built for action—simple, memorable and evocative. (p. 213)

Now, we get to the heart of the solution: "to address the idea-action gap *requires agents of transformation who are ready and willing to act in progressive ways*" (Perkins, 2003, p. 215; my emphasis). Agents of transformation are leaders who act in ways that produce others who act similarly.

Action poetry, says Perkins (2003), is in short supply, so we need to start with leveraging what we have. These new leaders (in very short supply at this time in education) have greater perspective in what is going on. Because of their developmental experience, they have a capacity to notice more, which "involves a receptive alertness rather than stand-back analysis" (p. 217):

> An ideal developmental leader tries to adopt progressive [inter-actions] regardless of what others are doing. When giving feedback, the person offers communicative rather than negative or conciliatory feedback. When collaborating with others to start a project, the person brings to the table not fully developed ideas but trial balloons or sacrificial plans held loosely to avoid the danger of early retrenchment. (p. 217)

Developmental leaders (Perkins's term; mine is the "new theoreticians" or "system thinkers in action") see the underlying patterns and "act visibly." They model the new actions. Thus "developmental leaders function as exemplars, facilitators, mentors within a group, helping to move it toward a progressive culture" (Perkins, 2003, p. 219).

In terms of leveraging change, Perkins (2003) talks about "the law of local impact" connecting with "the law of global impact":

The law of local impact: The influence of developmental leaders tends to be local, cultivating progressive practices most in groups directly involved with them. (Perkins, 2003, p. 222)

Whereas:

The law of global impact: Transformation toward a culture of progressive practice depends on a contact architecture [structure, roles, mechanisms] that mixes people enough to foster propagation of progressive practices from group to group . . . along with a critical mass of developmental leaders to seed the process. (Perkins, 2003, p. 224)

And the punch line:

Vision and policy from the top as well as formal training can help to foster the progressive transformation. They may be essential to getting it started. But they do not do the actual work of transformation. *This is done by the developmental leaders,* if people mix enough and there is a critical mass of such leaders. Such a transformation is a *system-level phenomenon,* one not so easily understood or appreciated. (Perkins, 2003, p. 224; emphases added)

Here, we have the essence of *Leadership & Sustainability:* the deliberate fostering of developmental leaders who act locally and beyond, all the while producing such leadership in others. It's an uphill battle to start with:

Simply acting progressively is not enough to cause other human beings in complex social contexts to catch on. The developmental leader needs to act not just progressively but with high visibility, not so much proselytizing as alerting, exposing, and explaining—raising consciousness casually in the natural flow of working together. (Perkins, 2003, p. 225)

When Steven Munby, Director of Evaluation and Lifelong Learning in the Knowsley District, England, talks about practicing "crafted gossip" (Chapter 6), he is talking precisely about developmental leadership of this kind. It is difficult, sophisticated, but it can be done. And can be done in a way that addresses both short-term and long-term results. You don't get this good overnight, and that is the point. Create schools and districts that give people an opportunity to practice developmental leadership and to leverage each other as they do. This is the road to sustainability.

We can see no greater confirmation that we are on the right track than when we see that the deeper work of Heifetz (2004), Perkins (2003), and Kegan and Lahey (2001) all lead to the same conclusion. We need fundamental changes in the cultures of organizations and systems; the new work is harder to do, requiring much more sophistication—leaders working to change conditions, including the development of other leaders to reach a critical mass. This is the new work of leaders for sustainability. King Arthur's roundtable has been set. Enter the new leaders, starting at the school level.

CHAPTER FIVE

Leadership at the School Level

I have spent some time setting the stage for school leadership because effective school leadership does not mean much unless it is cast in a context that matters. The particulars in this chapter concern how the principal (or school leadership) relates to teachers, students, parents, and the community and to other schools within *and* beyond the district.

The new work of school leaders is a mixture of technical and adaptive work. A technical problem would be teaching a child to read, or raising literacy proficiency scores from 57% to 75%, as was the case in England. Not that technical problems are easy to solve, but we do know how to approach them. An adaptive challenge is one in which we do not have the answers. Engaging alienated or unmotivated students, involving parents and the community at large, addressing social inclusion of special needs students, moving from 75% literacy to 90%, and reforming high schools are all examples of current adaptive problems.

If you want a shorthand criterion to determine whether a problem is technical or adaptive, try Heifetz's (2004) "the person with the problem is the problem, and the solution." Put another way, adaptive challenges require the deep participation of the people with the problem; that is why it is more complex and why it requires more sophisticated leadership.

School leaders need to keep working on technical problems. There is much more to be done in literacy and mathematics, for example. And recall our sixth sustainability component: dual commitment to both short-term and long-term outcomes. Technical problems are more amenable to short-term results and need to be constantly attended to. Adaptive challenges take longer and are more politically charged, as solutions are difficult to discern and learn, and some disequilibrium on the way to addressing the problem is inevitable.

I won't spend time in this chapter on the good technical work that schools need to do. We have written about this elsewhere (Fullan & Hargreaves, 1992). What I am saying is that even relatively advanced work such as creating professional learning communities does not push the adaptive envelope. It is necessary but not sufficient for sustainability. It's critical to do, but we need more. We need to keep this good work going as we drill down. Let's illustrate in reference to teachers and students, parents and the community, and relationships to other schools within and beyond the district.

ASSESSMENT FOR LEARNING

In the evolution of teaching and learning, we are still at the early stages. With developments in cognitive science and related fields, we are beginning to see what this new work entails. One of the most high-yield strategies that has come on the scene is "assessment for learning," high yield in the sense that it represents a powerful strategy for changing teaching and learning, and it is learnable within reasonable time frames (see Black et al., 2003; Hill & Crevola, 2003; Stiggins, 2001).

A by-product of external accountability, assessment for learning refers to "any assessment for which the first priority is to serve the purpose of promoting students' learning" (Black et al., 2003, p. 2). Black and his colleagues worked with 36 teachers of English and mathematics in six secondary schools in local education authorities in England. For Black et al., assessment for learning involved working with teachers to improve four areas of classroom teaching and learning: questioning, feedback through marking, peer- and self-assessment by students, and the formative use of summative tests (the latter being external accountability tests). We will get to the changes in practice in a moment. Even using external tests as the criterion, Black et al. documented improvements in the results of most teachers, which, "If replicated across the whole school they would raise the performance of a school at the 25th percentile of achievement nationally into the upper half" (p. 29).

Consider, however, the changes in practice and their effects on students and teachers. One of the four components of assessment literacy—peer- and self-assessment—has the powerful effect of increasing students' voice and motivation (Black et al., 2003):

> It is very difficult for students to achieve a learning goal unless they understand that goal and can assess what they need to do to reach it. So self-assessment is essential to learning. . . .
>
> In practice peer-assessment turns out to be an important complement and may even be a prior requirement for self-assessment. (pp. 49–50)

As one student put it:

> After a student marked my investigation, I can now acknowledge my mistakes easier. I hope that it is not just me who learnt from the investigation but the student who marked it did also. Next time I will have to make my explanations clearer, as they said, "it is hard to understand." . . . I will now explain my equation so it is clear. (Black et al., 2003, p. 66)

The affect of assessment for learning on the teacher-learner nexus is considerable:

> As the teachers came to listen more attentively to the students' responses they began to appreciate more fully that learning was not a process of passive reception of knowledge, but one in which the learners were active in creating their own understanding. . . . The teachers gradually developed learning environments that focused on improvement and this was achieved through evolving and supporting collaborative learning within their classrooms. (Black et al., 2003, p. 59)

As the project unfolded, many teachers moved away from the perception of their students as having fixed levels of ability. Teachers taught differently and expected (created environments for) students to take some responsibility for their own learning. As Black et al. (2003) say, "The students are the ones that have to do the learning; the teachers know that they cannot do the learning for the students" (p. 94). This is Heifetz's (2004) "the person with the problem is the problem and the solution." One teacher expressed his learning this way:

> It became obvious that one way to make *significant sustainable* change was to get the students doing more of the thinking. I then began to search for ways to make the learning process more transparent to the students. Indeed, I now spend my time looking for ways to get students to take responsibility for their learning at the same time making the learning more collaborative. (pp. 94–95; my emphasis)

This revolution in pedagogy is reinforced in Claxton's (2002) *Building Learning Power,* mentioned in Chapter 2. Recall his "four Rs" of learning power: resilience (being ready, absorbed, and persistent in learning); resourcefulness (learning in different ways); reflectiveness (becoming more strategic about learning); and reciprocity (able to learn alone and with others). Claxton provides many concrete examples of what these four Rs look like in practice, which amount to radically reculturing the way teachers teach and the way students learn, all of which is congruent with new breakthroughs in cognitive science (see Bereiter, 2002; National Research Council, 1999).

There are three conclusions for us. First, there is some, but not much, of this kind of teaching going on; second, if we can get more of it, we are on the road to sustainability (sustainable because it involves students and teachers working smarter, not harder—the work is easier because the labor is distributed and the learning is individual and socially engaging); third, it will take leadership to get a critical mass of this activity under way and continuing to move forward.

This breakthrough in pedagogy is not a quick fix, but as Black and others have found, teachers and students can make considerable progress within 2 years. More to our point, it will require whole-school, whole-district, whole-system leadership for the results to be realized: "The full potential for improvement can only be realized when students experience new ways of working consistently across all their classes" (Black et al., 2003, p. 101).

We have a way to go. Black et al. (2003) quote several studies, including the following:

> In none of the nine schools I visited had there been a decision to use targets in order to shift classroom practice and a school's

ethos away from didacticism and pupils' dependence on teachers, toward pupils' greater involvement in setting and assessment cf the tasks for themselves and in negotiation with their teachers. (Blanchard, 2002, p. 119)

Incidentally, schools with traditionally high scores on achievement tests are no better off. These "cruising schools," as Stoll and Fink (2002) call them, get good results because the students are good in the first place. They show no particular evidence that the teachers are good in the way that Black et al., (2003), Claxton (2002), and others are talking about. Indeed, high-achieving students on traditional academic tests do not make better organization or societal leaders, as we are seeing only too well in the political and corporate world.

Be that as it may, the role of the school leader is to help lead and facilitate the revolution in pedagogy so necessary for sustainable learning in individuals and organizations. They also need to tackle one of the most perplexing problems facing educational reform: how to understand and change the culture of the school for the better.

CHANGING SCHOOL CULTURES

Cultures consist of the shared values and beliefs in the organization. As the Hay Group (2004) observes in their study of school "cultures that learn," *culture* refers to the things that people "agree are true" and "agree are right." The Hay Group conducted a study of cultures in 134 secondary schools in England. It had access to the value-added student achievement data over the previous 3 years and were able to group the schools according to those that had relatively higher- and relatively lower-value-added performance over this period. And then it examined the cultures of the schools according to 30 statements of culture they had identified that might be associated with improvement. What it found was revealing.

Teachers in the schools were asked to rank order the 30 traits in a hierarchy. In the "high-valued-added schools," the top six traits were (Hay Group, 2004)

- Measuring and monitoring targets and results
- A hunger for improvement—high hopes and expectations

- Raising capability—helping people learn—laying foundations for later success
- Focusing on value added—holding hope for every child— every gain a victory
- Promoting excellence—pushing the boundaries for achievement—world class
- Making sacrifices to put pupils first (p. 33).
- (Working together—learning from each other—was a close seventh)

In the "low-value-added" cultures, the top six were

- Measuring and monitoring targets and test results
- Warmth, humor—repartee—feet on the ground
- Recognizing personal circumstances—making allowances— toleration—it's the effort that counts
- Keeping up with initiatives—doing what is required— following policy
- Creating a pleasant and collegial working environment
- Working together—learning from each other—sharing resources and ideas—investing in others (Hay Group, 2004, p. 35).

There are many more nuances in the interpretation of the results than I am able to take up here, but note that the successful schools had a much more demanding culture (one of my themes in this book)— hunger for improvement, promoting excellence, holding hope for every child—while the less successful schools had less of a press on improvement and were more forgiving if results were not forthcoming— recognizing personal circumstances (it's the effort that counts), warmth/humor, and pleasant and collegial working environments.

As the Hay Group (2004) concludes, measurement and monitoring is a way of life in all of England's schools. And it was not that warmth/humor and pleasant working environments were missing in the successful schools, only that they were not ranked as high as the hunger-for-improvement press. The trait "working together— learning from each other" was just below the top tier of characteristics of the more successful schools. One can think of working together as powerful, but only when other high-demand elements are in place. In other words, there has to be some driving focus to what people are interacting about.

Put differently, the *bottom* (i.e., those elements least valued) six characteristics for high-value-added schools were

1. Preventing mistakes

2. Respecting professional autonomy

3. Respecting privacy

4. Admitting you don't know

5. Investing time with those who can achieve the most

6. Admitting mistakes

Whereas the least valued characteristics in the lower-performing schools were

1. Respecting privacy

2. Single-minded dedication

3. Keeping promises

4. The school comes first

5. Promoting excellence

6. Preventing mistakes

The above findings should not be interpreted too literally, because we are looking at one preliminary study and culture is a complex concept. For example, schools pushing for excellence in a no-excuses manner with a fear of admitting mistakes can become extreme places to work. It may also be the case that a high-demand culture may cause student achievement scores to increase in the short run but not over the long haul (the plateauing problem). Longer-term, sustainable reform requires the deep ownership of teachers and principals.

My main point, to return to Perkins (2003), is that effective cultures establish more and more progressive interactions in which demanding processes produce both good ideas and social cohesion. A sense of moral purpose is fueled by a focus on value-added high expectations for all, raising capability, pulling together, and an ongoing hunger for improvement.

Changing school cultures for the better is difficult but not impossible. Some of this can be done through capacity-building training that fosters and embeds professional learning communities. The Hay Group recommends comparing actual versus ideal cultures and working on the discrepancies. Of course, this whole book is about changing school cultures through new leadership at all levels. It requires, as I argue throughout, much more sophisticated leadership and more difficult learning than schools have hitherto been engaged in. All the issues of establishing new forms of "demanding trust" are also at play (see Bryk & Schneider, 2002; A. Hargreaves, 2002; Reina & Reina, 1999). Still, sustainability is very much a matter of changes in culture: powerful strategies that enable people to question and alter certain values and beliefs as they create new forms of learning within and between schools, and across levels of the system.

PARENTS AND THE COMMUNITY

In all of our work with schools and districts, the question of how best to relate to parents and the community is right up there with changing school cultures on the scale of difficulty. The key to addressing this is indirect as well as direct. Indirectly, when a school has its act together, that is, when leaders and teachers as a group have the collective capacity to make improvements, they become more confident and proactive in seeking parent and community connections that support classroom and school work.

Bryk and Schneider's (2002) study of the consequences of high- and low-trust schools in Chicago is a case in point. They found that some schools (usually due to school leadership) developed cultures of trust (defined as "relational trust," consisting of respect, competence, personal regard for others, and integrity). In low-trust schools,

Teachers criticized parents for their lack of interest in education, family drug dependency, and unemployment. They complained that much in their students' home structures impeded learning, and they took a generally dim view of the quality of parenting that was occurring. (p. 48)

In high-trust schools (similarly disadvantaged community, but different school cultures),

Teachers constantly spoke about the importance of respecting parents, regardless of their background or education achievement. . . . Although many students came from troubled homes, teachers did not attempt to distance themselves from their students or their families. (Bryk & Schneider, 2002, p. 84)

And,

Teachers' active encouragement of parents, coupled with their demonstrated personal regard for the children, opened up possibilities for teachers and parents to negotiate complementary roles in the children's education. (p. 86)

As Bryk and Schneider (2002) emphasize, under conditions of power asymmetry with poor parents, vulnerable and unconfident in their relationship to schools, it is incumbent on principals and teachers to reach out, be empathetic, and create possibilities for parent involvement. When they do, as Bryk and Schneider found, greater connection is made with parents and students, and achievement goes up.

Principal and teacher capacity and confidence are all the more important with middle-class parents. Here, it is the *parents* who are more often experienced as threatening. A collective sense of efficacy on the part of the school puts them in a position to be proactive and nondefensive. This applies to technical work, such as parent workshops on how to relate to homework (middle-class parents are equally at sea on this one) or to adaptive challenges, such as how to do collective assessment for learning among teachers and how to pursue Claxton's (2002) "building learning power." Claxton, in fact, has a number of suggestions for relating to parents, such as helping parents foster children's questioning spirit, discussing with parents the new ideas for learning, and so on.

All of this applies to the schools' adaptive challenges in relating to the broader community, integrating and coordinating the work of social service agencies with the school as a hub, getting the support of community leaders, relating to city or local councils, and forming partnerships with business and labor groups.

To take one example, Pedro Noguera (2003) makes a disturbing and compelling case for what schools and communities face in improving urban schools in the United States. He argues that "until there is a genuine commitment to address the social context of schooling—to confront the 'urban condition'—it will be impossible to bring about significant and sustainable improvements in urban public schools" (p. 6). Noguera tackles a number of fundamental problems, including addressing racial inequality, curbing violence inside and outside the school, motivating alienated youth, and increasing social capital among parents and the community. These are all overwhelming problems, but Noguera shows how schools and communities can partner to work differently. He makes our systems point by, in effect, claiming that we need educators and community members who can broaden their perspective in action:

> Unless increased pressure [on schools] is accompanied by systemic changes in the way schools respond to the needs of students and parents, and genuine assistance is provided to the schools serving the neediest children, it is unlikely that lasting, significant change will be made. (p. 96)

More than a radical critic of the present situation, Noguera, (2003) concludes that educators, including himself, must work on practical solutions. He provides several directional strategies. They represent complex work and, in fact, exemplify system thinkers in action. Noguera is one of the "new theoreticians."

To conclude, working with communities to bring about sustainable reform represents a set of complex adaptive challenges having all the attributes that Heifetz (2004) identifies. The solutions have to be worked out with the stakeholders, and to do this requires skilled, confident school leaders, who have one foot in the present and the other on the sustainability accelerator.

STEPPING OUT

All of this would be impossible if a school leader arrived at the doorstep and was expected to do so from scratch. It will work only if school leaders can find and interact with peers working to address the same adaptive problems; if school districts are providing developmental experiences and ongoing support for principals and others (Chapter 6); and if large systems are designing strategies and investing resources intended to give leaders opportunities to develop their capacities to practice and consolidate system thinking in action (Chapter 7).

Opportunities for lateral and vertical capacity building through networks and partnerships must abound if we are to get and keep the critical mass of leaders to do this kind of work and to do so in a way that continually regenerates leadership for the future. As we will see, this is not a matter of bombarding the system with network-based strategies, which may add to overload and confusion rather than focused application. At the end of the day, leadership for sustainability requires a fair degree of discipline and focus.

We are still at the school level, and the message is twofold. First, school leaders have the obligation to seek out and be responsive to opportunities to practice system thinking in action with other school leaders in structured initiatives within and beyond the district, including working with students, parents, and community leaders. School leaders should know what they are looking for: focused, sustained experiences that enable them to develop the core concepts and skills that we have been discussing in this chapter. Second, it won't work for the system as a whole unless individuals and groups equally commit to sharing and helping others develop. Sustainable learning is a two-way street. It is time for school leaders to step out, because in the absence of this, they have no possibility of furthering their own and others' system-thinking-doing capacities.

CHAPTER SIX

Leadership at the District Level

When it comes to sustainability, each level above you helps or hinders (it is rarely neutral). Just as the teacher is affected by the culture of the school, the school is affected by the culture of the district or the region. It is possible for a school to become highly collaborative despite the district that it is in, but it is not possible to *stay* highly collaborative in these circumstances. The district role can foster continuous improvement of schools, or it can take its toll on continuity through neglect or misguided policy actions. The leadership requirements at the district level are much more complex than the ones we saw in Chapter 5 because a larger part of the system is being led in the direction of sustainability.

We have lost quite a lot of time over the past few decades by flipping back and forth from centralization to decentralization (if you are in this business long enough, you can get hit by the same pendulum more than once). Many jurisdictions have promoted (and some still are promoting) site-based management on the assumption that the local school is where it counts, so support should go directly to the school. In many cases, deliberate strategies from the state level have played down or bypassed the district. If you have your systems hat on, you know right away that this is a mistake. You cannot omit any part of the system without paying the price.

Some of the principles of site-based management still apply: greater empowerment at the school level, more control over budget, and acceptance of accountability, for instance. But there are two core reasons why districts or comparable regional structures are essential. First, decentralized schools will have variable capacities to engage in continuous improvement, and therefore some agency has to be responsible for helping develop capacity and for intervening (with a goal to developing capacity) when performance is low. The second reason is even more fundamental for sustainability: We can't change the system without lateral (cross-school and cross-district) sharing and capacity development. It is very much the district's role to help make the latter happen.

We have been working with several districts in Canada, the United States, and the United Kingdom to help develop capacity building across the district as a first step toward sustainability. In this chapter, I briefly review the lessons from this work to once again demonstrate that powerful abstract concepts can and must be evident in strategic practice. These lessons are followed by a case review of a district in order to illustrate the systemic nature of this work. Finally, I revisit sustainability.

LESSONS LEARNED

We recently completed a review of our district work and linked it to other findings in the literature (Fullan, Bertani, & Quinn, 2004). Ten key lessons stood out:

1. Leading with a compelling, driving conceptualization

2. Collective moral purpose

3. The right bus

4. Capacity building

5. Lateral capacity building

6. Ongoing learning

7. Productive conflict

8. A demanding culture

9. External partners

10. Growing financial investments

The lessons do not adequately address sustainability. They overlap, but not completely, with the eight conditions for sustainability. Think of these 10 elements as preconditions for sustainability. No districts have yet to engage in sustainability with any depth, largely because the larger system is not working on it. But this new work does represent a strong step in the right direction.

1. Leading With a Compelling, Driving Conceptualization

Deep district reform requires leaders at or near the top who understand the direction in which the district needs to go and are sophisticated about how to get there (which does not mean front-end crystal clarity). Basically, what they need is an understanding of and continual learning orientation to the 10 lessons we are about to discuss. In the absence of leaders who can steer and facilitate the evolving direction on a daily basis, no amount of external pressure and support will make a lasting difference. In short, these leaders are system thinkers in action who foster other system thinkers within the district.

Understanding the concepts is critical because they are powerful, but they are also abstract and difficult to grasp unless one is immersed in their application. We find that the terms travel easily—*professional learning communities, networks, capacity building,* and so on—but the meaning of the underlying concepts does not. Icebergs don't travel well if you are just trying to move the visible part. Many leaders try to take shortcuts by slicing off the visible part of the iceberg, assuming they have captured its full power.

As these leaders pursue the depth of change, they must build a coalition of leaders. Like distributed leadership at the school level, large-scale reform requires pluralized leadership, with teams of people creating and driving a clear, coherent strategy. Having a driving conceptualization means high engagement with others in the district and plenty of two-way communication, which deepens shared ownership and commitment at all levels of the district. Leaders improve their conceptualization through the interactive feedback that comes from application and corresponding reflection and continuous refinement.

2. Collective Moral Purpose

The moral purpose of educators may seem universal, but it has too often emerged as an individual phenomenon: the heroic teacher, principal, or superintendent who succeeds for brief periods of time against all odds. This moral martyrdom is great for the individual soul, but it does not lead to sustainable reform. We need instead to think of the moral imperative as an organizational or system quality (see Fullan, 2003b).

To recall our definition of moral purpose, it consists of (a) a commitment to raising the bar and closing the gap of student achievement for all individuals and schools; (b) a commitment to treat people ethically—adults and students alike (which does not mean being soft; see Lesson 8, on demanding cultures); and (c) a commitment to improving the whole district, not just one's own school.

In the districts we are talking about, district leaders constantly communicate the moral purpose. They make it clear that everyone has a responsibility for changing the larger education context for the better. These leaders foster a culture in which school principals become "almost" as concerned about the success of other schools in the district as they are about their own. They know that competition among schools within districts leads to counterproductive behaviors—what Pfeffer and Sutton (2000) refer to as "internal competition [that] turns friends into enemies" (p. 180), thereby undermining interdependence, trust, and loyalty. Cultivating identity beyond one's own school to other schools in the district is an act of system thinking that contributes to changes in the overall context toward greater sustainability. As in all successful organizations, the "cause" is more important than quotas or targets.

3. The Right Bus

In his discussion of great companies, Jim Collins (2001) talks about the critical importance of getting the right people on the right bus and in the right seats, and the wrong people off the bus. Here, we take one step back and ask: What is the right bus (structures and roles)? The lesson from our districts is that some reorganization of roles is necessary so that there is a laser-like focus on teaching and learning, building professional learning communities and partnerships, and, especially, so that the normal "distractors"—managerial issues, crises, and so on—are handled in a way that do not take school and system leaders constantly away from the focus on students and learning.

Setting up and maintaining an effective structure involves much more than the typical organization chart. It means identifying and cultivating a coalition of leaders. Basically, it means a core group of leaders who share a commitment to and skills in developing the other nine lessons in action in a concerted way. A key reminder is that structure is not enough. You have to couple reculturing and restructuring.

4. Capacity Building

New structures are sterile without corresponding capacity building for those inhabiting the new roles. This is where building the new culture comes in. In complex, uncertain environments, where roles are often not well coordinated (in other words, in schools and school systems), a major, explicit effort is required to develop new capacities, which, above all, involve capacities to work together. Districts in the forefront of development promote "learning in context"—not just through workshops but also through daily interactions in cultures designed for job-embedded learning.

In Chicago, for example, people learn in weekly meetings, study groups, focused institutes, and walk-through site visits, in which teams visit schools to learn from and react to leadership and teaching and learning strategies. These comprehensive, multiyear strategies involve school teams and district level leaders in weeklong institutes and multiple-day follow-ups. The transfer of skills and ideas to classrooms and schools is enhanced by cycles of application and regular examination of student results.

Capacity building, as I said, is an abstract concept, and it is easy to get it wrong. It is not just workshops and professional development for all. It is the daily habit of *working together,* and you can't learn this from a workshop or course. You need to learn it by doing it and having mechanisms for getting better at it on purpose.

Finally, capacity building means constantly developing leadership for the future. There is plenty of turnover in systems these days, and as I said earlier, it is not turnover, per se, that is the problem, but rather discontinuity of direction. Because sustaining districts foster leaders who also develop other leaders, there is a constant pool and pipeline of people who can push further and deeper.

5. Lateral Capacity Building

Closely aligned with capacity building for roles and teams within schools is the discovery of the power of learning from a wider group of peers across schools (and later, we will see, across districts). Lateral capacity building has the double advantage of accessing more ideas while increasing people's identification with a larger piece of the system—again, system thinking in action (of course, it depends on the substance and depth of learning).

In York Region District, just north of Toronto, Canada, school teams from 105 schools meet with us 7 days a year to learn from each other with respect to leadership, developing learning communities, and creating greater coherence, all in the service of improving student learning. Between sessions, they are busy creating new cultures of learning within and across schools.

In England, the Bristol Local Education Authority is using lateral capacity building to improve its 19 secondary schools. The high schools in Bristol include 10 that are above the national norms on various measures of performance and 9 that are below. During the past year, the district leadership and the 19 principals have collectively developed an improvement plan that pairs schools and departments in order to learn how to raise the bar and close the gap of student achievement. To take one example, a group of teachers in one math department who have been successful in motivating otherwise disengaged students work with students in other math departments who are facing similar problems, with much success. They share syllabuses, examine teaching strategies together, use assessment of student work for learning, and so on.

Think of our systems criterion: If you are a secondary school principal in Bristol sitting around a table with others as you engage in cross-school development, you realize that you are not just in an initiative to improve your own school, but that you are part of an attempt to improve the set of secondary schools in Bristol. If all or most of the 19 principals think this way, you have an increment in system thinking and therefore increase the chances of system transformation. Bristol is at the early stages of this complex endeavor and is having some difficulty moving forward after a strong start. It is too early to tell how successful it will be, but the strategy is aimed in the right direction.

There are many other examples of lateral capacity building in this book (e.g., Chapters 2 and 7). It is a powerful, high-yield strategy because it mobilizes commitment and new ideas on the ground.

6. Ongoing Learning

All districts that improve are committed to and have many mechanisms for learning as they go. This learning focuses on at least two related aspects: Are people learning and satisfied/energized, and should the policy, strategy, structure, and roles be altered based on feedback from experience?

With respect to learning and energy, a large focus is on "assessment for learning" (Black et al., 2003; Stiggins, 2001). When done well, this is one of the most powerful high-leverage strategies for improving student learning that we know of. Educators *collectively* at the school and district levels become more skilled and focused at assessing, disaggregating, and using student achievement as a tool for ongoing improvement.

In terms of satisfaction and energy, effective districts need to take the pulse of student engagement, principal and teacher ownership and morale, parent and community satisfaction, and so on. As part of the new "intelligent accountability" framework that I referred to in Chapter 2, the new evaluation work will involve developing the capacity and procedures for school-based self-review as it relates to internal development—work that will involve the district interacting with schools.

The other absolutely crucial aspect of learning concerns the ongoing assessment of whether the policies and strategies are working or if they need improvement. Because these districts are so engaged on a daily basis, problems are picked up naturally in the culture. From our change process knowledge, we know that it is a mistake to abandon plans too soon when difficulties are encountered. One has to attempt to work through the implementation dips. But engaged districts know the difference between a dip and a chasm. When serious problems are experienced in a variety of situations and when they persist or get worse, involved districts pick up the cues early and act on them, sometimes by tweaking the approach, other times by reconsidering certain policies or strategies. As we have seen, they learn from mistakes.

7. Productive Conflict

All changes worth their salt reveal differences. Because districtwide reform is complex and involves many levels and people, it produces questions and disagreements. Successful districts must engage in a difficult balancing act. If they give in too soon in the face of conflict and fail to stay the course, they will not be able to work through the inevitable barriers to implementation. But if they show an inflexible commitment to a vision—even if it is based on passionate moral purpose—they can drive resistance underground and miss essential lessons until it is too late.

As district leaders get better at continuous improvement, they learn to distinguish good conflict from bad. Built-in checks and balances of data-driven reform help sort out productive from dysfunctional conflict. Successful organizations explicitly value differences and do not panic when things go wrong. Pfeffer and Sutton (2000) found that organizations learn from mistakes while still being disciplined about what they are learning.

Successful districts are collaborative, but they are not always congenial and consensual. Working in a high-trust yet demanding culture, participants take disagreements as normal when undergoing changes, and are able to value and work through differences.

Some commitments are nonnegotiable, such as raising the bar and closing the gap, ongoing development of professional capacity, and transparency of results. The nonnegotiables reduce the areas of conflict and channel differences into areas that are essential for solving problems.

8. A Demanding Culture

Organizations with high levels of trust among participants combine respect, personal regard, integrity, and competence—yes, competence (Bryk & Schneider, 2002). We cannot trust even well-intentioned people if they are not good at what they are doing. Effective, highly interactive cultures incorporate high pressure and high support; it is impossible not to notice whether someone is doing great work or bad work. Because people in these cultures know that improvement is tough going and that disagreement is a normal part of any change, they are more inclined and prepared to confront it.

As Bryk and Schneider (2002) found in studying high-trust school cultures in Chicago, these cultures are more—not less—likely to take action against persistently uncaring or incompetent teachers. They take action not just because an uncaring teacher is bad for the students but also because failure to act can poison the whole atmosphere. Students, parents, and colleagues know when bad teaching is being tolerated.

Low-trust cultures do not have the capacity to engage in the great effort and difficult work of improvement. High-trust cultures make the extraordinary possible, energizing people and giving them the wherewithal to be successful under enormously demanding conditions—and the confidence that staying the course will pay off. Recall also our discussion in the previous chapter of the Hay Group (2004) study of "cultures for learning." School cultures associated with improvement were far more demanding than other cultures.

Bryk and Schneider (2002) and the Hay Group (2004) are talking about high-trust schools; we are talking about raising the bar to provide *high-trust districts* in which many schools are motivated and supported to engage in demanding work, able to withstand frustrations along the way, and persist in their efforts to make reform doable and worthwhile.

9. External Partners

All improving districts that we know about have active partners— such as business groups, foundations, community-based organizations, universities, networks, federations—that help build districts' professional capacity. Unfortunately, we also know of districts that have strong external partners and additional resources and are going nowhere. If leaders don't have the other nine crucial components for district reform in operation, external partners simply exacerbate overload and fragmentation. When local capacity is low, the role of external partners is to help build initial capacity. When local capacity is high, we find that districts are proactive and selective users of external partners.

Well-placed pressure from external partners, combined with internal energy, can be the stimulus for tackling something that might not otherwise be addressed, and district leaders can use this to stir the pot in purposeful directions.

In the following chapter, I will consider the use of networks from the system perspective, where some jurisdictions are using peer-related partnerships with a variety of agencies in order to stimulate further reform.

10. Growing Financial Investments

We have learned that governments are willing to put more money into public education—not just because of the need but also because they perceive that the investment pays off. Last year's success is next year's new money.

Districts need to take two steps to increase financial investment. First, they need to redeploy existing resources in the service of capacity building, focusing on teaching and learning. In Chicago, over the past 2 years, the district has reallocated resources to double the investment in the Reading Initiative.

Districts also need to figure out how to give responsive local and central governing bodies the confidence to risk investing additional money: the confidence that the investments will pay off morally and politically through improved performance.

Sustaining districts, in short, are resource hungry. They seek and attract resources and know how to use them for best effect, which creates a virtuous resource cycle.

While each of these 10 lessons is grounded in the reality of districts with whom we are working, they can still be somewhat abstract. Before returning to sustainability, per se, I consider a case example to further illustrate the nature of district work that attempts to pave the way toward greater sustainability.

A CASE EXAMPLE: KNOWSLEY LOCAL EDUCATION AUTHORITY, ENGLAND

Knowsley Local Education Authority (LEA) (school district) is a metropolitan authority just east of Liverpool. It is defined as the sixth-most deprived authority in England; more than 79% of residents live in the most deprived 10% wards in England. The LEA consists of 59 primary schools, 11 secondary schools, and 7 special schools, with a total student population of 28,000 and 1,500 professional staff. Knowsley has considerably higher levels of social and economic disadvantage than the national average. Unemployment is high, and income levels are low. For many years, there has been a culture of low aspiration and low self-esteem. Historically, student achievement is low, and the take-up of further education is poor.

In 1999, Knowsley LEA was audited or inspected as part of the regular cycle of inspections conducted by OFSTED (Office for Standards in Education). The 1999 assessment found weaknesses on most basic dimensions of performance: student achievement, capacity to improve, relationships between the LEA and schools, and linkage to the community. A secondary inspection was conducted in 2003. In effect the question is: Can a low-performing, complex, and difficult district improve significantly within 4 short years? It did (see OFSTED's, 2003a, assessment). And it did so by using in a comprehensive way many of the ideas we have been talking about in this book. Let's take a look at what the district accomplished, and then how they went about it.

First, what were the changes in performance between 1999 and 2003? I paraphrase and quote from the OFSTED (2003a) inspection report:

Recent developments and the implementation of well thought through initiatives have resulted in Knowsley establishing itself as an LEA of some significance. It has improved over the past three years and shown how vision and leadership together with excellent relationships with schools, can revive an education service. (p. 2)

More particularly (OF STED, 2003a),

Primary school standards are rising faster than the national rate of improvement. In 1999, Knowsley's rate of achievement for 11-year-olds in literacy was 64% compared to 71% in 2003; for numeracy the figures are 64% and 69%, respectively; this at a time when national scores were flat-lined. (p. 2)

The number of pupils continuing in full time education improved significantly . . . from 50 to 62%. (p. 6)

Only student achievement at secondary schools—a problem everywhere—was found wanting. Pupils' attainment is unsatisfactory but improving in secondary schools. (p. 2)

Between 2000 and 2003, Knowsley's scores for the percentage of students achieving passing grades in advanced subjects (a measure of secondary school improvement in England) increased from 25% in 2000 to 33.7% in 2003, after virtually no improvement in the previous 4 years. This increase is higher than the national rate of improvement over the same 3-year period.

Funding from external sources has improved dramatically, as much following success as causing it (remember our "growing financial investments"). In 2002/2003, external funding was £33.6 million, or 28% of the total spent, compared with £8.7 million, or 10% in 1999/ 2000 (OFSTED, 2003a, p. 8).

In other parts of the inspection report, OFSTED (2003a) comments on several of the system quality accomplishments (which begin to get at how the LEA did it):

> Changes in staff at the [borough] council level and amongst key partners have made this a very different authority, operating in a new way from that inspected in 1999. The director of education . . . most of the leadership and management team, the team of school improvement officers and many of the special education needs (SEN) and social inclusion staff have all joined the department within the last four years [reminiscent of getting the right people on the bus]. The new administration has developed further the existing strengths in partnerships and collaborative working and has taken them to an unusually high level. *Headteachers of individual schools see themselves as part of a wider team with responsibility for the education service throughout the borough.* (p. 2; my emphasis)

> Together with schools, they have embarked upon a series of carefully considered and very well-funded initiatives that are intended to transform education. . . . The productive partnership with schools goes beyond the changes being wrought at the classroom level. They characterise the authority's new approach to challenge, monitoring and interaction, underpin the framework for continuous professional development and are the foundation for a rigorous programme of school self-review. (p. 2)

> Monitoring arrangements are thorough. They are based on a detailed analysis of performance data, visits to and contacts with schools undertaken by school improvement officers and other officers of the LEA, and [monitoring is based] increasingly on the outcomes of school reviews. (p. 14)

> The last inspection found that the LEA's provision of performance data to schools was inadequate. This is much improved and schools are provided in a timely way with good sets of performance data along with advice and training on how to use these to support improvement. *This is now a strength of the LEA.* (p. 14; my emphasis)

Such "assessment for learning," observes OFSTED (2003a), has applied to all schools but has been additionally effective with respect to improving schools that need extra help and with special education and social inclusion of pupils in the borough.

Finally, from the OFSTED (2003a) report:

The leadership of LEA officers is particularly good. They have raised the profile of education, clearly identified what more needs to be done, are effective in challenging schools, but also take care to highlight and celebrate success. This approach secures very strong support from schools. . . . The Comprehensive Performance Assessment (CPA), published in December 2002, gave the education service two stars for current performance and three stars (the highest grading) for its capacity to make further improvement. This inspection reinforces the latter judgement. (p. 4)

The above represents an objective assessment from an external authority. But let us now consider the strategy from the perspective of the Director of Education, Steve Munby and his colleagues. Notice the language, starting with the title of a document describing the purpose and strategy of the reform: "Broad and Deep: A Whole Authority Approach to Motivation and Learning, the Knowsley Transformation Strategy" (Munby, 2003)

Munby states that the drivers for change are low student performance, new leadership, external funding, and narrowing the gap between the highest- and lowest-performing schools.

Under "Managing Change," Munby (2003) points to "common moral purpose and shared principles; combining boldness with implementation strategy, [and] partnership—managing change together" (p. 1). He then refers to a teaching and learning strategy to focus on powerful learning: "establishing and sustaining the optimum mind state for learning and meeting the human mind's need for novelty, challenge, meaningmaking and feedback in learning" (p. 1). This is far more than literacy and numeracy scores, even though these short-term results remain a priority.

Munby then lists (note the language) "Priorities for Sustainability," which include the following:

- Establishing an innovative, coherent, and comprehensive policy framework that provides direction for school learning and teaching policy development
- The training of Lead Learners (LLs)
- Key LLs supporting clusters of primary and special schools to embed practice
- Continued cluster-based networks—action learning, describing and sharing practice, supporting small-scale action research to provide evidence of impact on pupil motivation, engagement with the learning process
- Encouragement and support of the further development and embedding of a culture of co-planning, co-teaching, co-review, and co-coaching in schools—everyone a leader of learning (p. 2)

Beyond this short list, there are a number of partnerships, a focus on social inclusion, and linkage to the community and the borough.

In a summary statement,

Knowsley's policy is to use collaborative working to drive systemwide reform and to change the role and function of the LEA itself. A big focus is the mechanism and children's agenda—promoting mutual accountability and binding schools to collective targets. Key factors underpinning this include:

- Moral purpose
- Leadership in the big picture
- The LEA as facilitator and relationship builder
- Frequent sampling of environment—"crafted gossip"—constantly checking out, reflecting and moving the dialogue forward
- Incentivising inclusion and reform
- Investing time and resources (Munby, 2003, p. 3)

This would be rhetoric if Knowsley had not already done a lot of this. There is much more to be done—but could there be a better concrete example of what I have called "the new theoretician" or "system thinkers in action": moral purpose, big picture, relationship building new and far, monitoring and adjusting approaches, and investing time and resources? And all of this is represented not just by the director of education but by the proliferation of leaders at all levels, and the fact that schools across the borough have bought into the overall plan and their part in it. School leaders too are thinking of the bigger picture, thereby changing the very system or context within which they work.

Knowsley is just one of a growing number of districts that is tackling deeper districtwide reform. I have already mentioned York Region, just north of Toronto, which is engaged in creating greater coherence and focus in all of its more than 170 schools, with a growing sense of shared identity and commitment on the part of teachers, principals, and district staff. Similarly, Guilford County Schools, in Greensboro, North Carolina, is developing strong districtwide reform in its 115 schools. In all of these cases, the focus is on raising the bar and closing the gap of student achievement, treating people with demanding respect, and contributing to the social environment in which schools work with each other and with their communities to bring about comprehensive improvements.

SUSTAINABILITY REVISITED

Four points: First, we are still talking about the early steps of sustainability. Some districts have moved forward, but even the best are likely to hit the "ceiling effect"—achievement goes up, but only to a point where it levels off.

Second, to go beyond this plateau, districts will need to pursue the sustainability agenda. Some of the districts from which we derived the 10 lessons are doing so; certainly, Knowsley is more explicitly committed in this direction. There is, of course, a significant overlap between these 10 lessons and the eight elements of sustainability from Chapter 2. But at this point, there is insufficient attention being paid to several of the sustainability elements: intelligent accountability, deep learning, cyclical energizing, and the long lever of leadership (see Chapter 2).

Third, the evolution of districtwide reform must continually grapple with reconciling the centralization-decentralization dilemma. It is critical not to err on one side or the other. Knowsley has evidential success that both levels can be combined in common pursuit. On the other hand, Ouchi (2003), as we saw in Chapter 1, argues forcefully that we need "to uproot the top-down way of doing things and replace it with huge, revolutionary change," including "every principal is an entrepreneur" and "every school controls its own budget" (pp. 13–14). I accept aspects of this direction but stress three additional factors arising from our sustainability framework: (1) the district has a critical role in helping to develop *school capacity* to act in more autonomous ways (Ouchi does not use the term *capacity* in his entire book); (2) successful districts, as we have seen, foster cross-school (and beyond) learning—lateral capacity building, which has powerful benefits for individual schools and the system as a whole (indeed, this is one way in which "systems" change toward sustainability); and (3) local school autonomy does not guarantee that underperforming schools will improve—districts have a moral (and increasingly legal) obligation to intervene in these schools.

Finally, and here we head toward Chapter 7, it is not possible for districts to move forward over time if the larger system is not a partner in fostering the sustainability agenda. The districts we have been talking about have a stronger chance to keep going for a while because they invest in leadership throughout the district, increasing chances that there will be continuity of direction (but school boards, especially in the United States, are volatile, with discontinuity being the norm). One positive sign is that districts like Knowsley and York Region recognize that their futures are not just a matter of internal development, but rather lie in partnering with wider networks. If the state, in turn, thinks through sustainability, it will know that its role must dramatically change. States need to provide more direct leadership for establishing the eight elements of sustainability, including leveraging the considerable capacities that already exist in many schools and districts.

CHAPTER SEVEN

Leadership at the System Level

I f the key to the future success is the increase of system thinking in action, system leaders have a dual role. One is to make system coherence more and more evident and accessible, the other is to foster interactions—horizontally and vertically—that promote system thinking in others. They also have to engage in a highly sophisticated balancing act. On one hand, there need to be strategies and resources devoted to the exploration of solutions to adaptive challenges. This is a politician's nightmare because it provides no clear answers at the beginning of the process. On the other hand, they must regularly focus on solutions. This is a practitioner's nightmare: hard hierarchies that push for and impose solutions.

If they are successful at turning the ship around, system leaders are helped by the presence and involvement of more and more school and district leaders of the kind discussed in Chapters 5 and 6.

NETWORKING AND INTELLIGENT ACCOUNTABILITY

I frame the problem of system leadership around two competing (but not necessarily mutually exclusive) strategies, which I will call "networking" and "intelligent accountability." Let's start with the former, because it is increasingly coming on the scene. It has its strengths, especially with respect to lateral capacity and increments of system thinking, and its weaknesses when it comes to converting good ideas into sustained actions.

England, as we saw earlier, is investing considerably in new "networked learning communities": school heads learning from each other, consortia of districts exchanging ideas, and clusters of groups and individuals attempting to create professional learning communities in place of the isolating effects of narrow-minded competition. More than 100 such networks have been founded over the past 2 years by the National College of School Leadership (NCSL). As stated in a main document,

> Networked Learning Communities are capitalizing and celebrating the diversity which exists within the system. By working in interdependent and mutually supportive ways, groups of schools have formed learning networks and are using diversity within and across schools as a positive force for knowledge-sharing and innovation. . . .
>
> As . . . professional energy and creativity is unleashed, schools are evolving into dynamic learning communities. . . . Networked Learning Communities are taking hold of the education agenda, focusing on values of partnership and collaboration *to create coherence* within the ever changing educational landscape. (2003b, p. 2; my emphasis)

Two other illustrations, and then we will come back to the matter of the strengths and weaknesses of network strategies, including the claim "to create coherence."

Godin (2001) writes about the power of "unleashing the idea virus." As Gladwell observes in the foreword, Godin's argument is that most successful ideas "are those that spread and grow because of the customer's [read 'practitioner's'] relationship to other customers—not the marketer's [read 'central government's'] to the customer" (p. 13).

Godin (2001) puts it this way:

> Marketing by interrupting people isn't cost effective anymore. You can't afford to seek out people and send them unwanted marketing messages, in large groups, and hope that some will send you money [read "implement your policies"].
>
> Instead the future belongs to marketers who establish a foundation and process where interested people can market to

each other. Ignite consumer networks and then get out of the way and let them talk. (p. 15; emphasis in original)

Don't get excited by the reference to "get out of the way"; let's stick with the metaphor for a moment. Godin (2001) says, "Give people a reason to listen and then create an infrastructure that will amplify their ability to spread word of mouth" (p. 46).

For our purposes, Godin is saying to system leaders, temper your tendency to innovate or make policy by *interruption.* He is not against it on moral or value grounds, just that it is a waste of money—it doesn't work. Again, in our terms, we might confine policy-by-interruption to those situations where schools are persistently failing. System level leaders have a moral obligation to intervene explicitly and directly in cases where schools are failing children. Even addressing this technical problem requires the wise use of authoritative direction and new capacity building. As necessary as this is, it doesn't get us anywhere on the sustainability agenda. For that to happen, people need to be engaged, not interrupted.

A second illustration is one I have used before concerning robins and titmice. DeGues (1997) takes up the story from biologist Alan Wilson's work on how innovation spreads among birds. Around 1900, when milk was first delivered to homes in England, both robins and titmice began to get inside the thin caps in order to drink the cream that floated to the top. In response, dairy distributors began putting aluminum seals on the bottles. Individual robins and titmice figured out how to pierce the seals to access the cream. The solution spread across the entire titmice community, but not so for robins.

Wilson found the answer. Titmice communicate. They fly from place to place in flocks of 8 to 10, with some change of membership. As individual birds or combinations found the answer, it was seen, learned, and adopted across the whole group. Robins are territorial. They stake out their ground and defend it in an antagonistic manner. Any good ideas (or bad for that matter) were confined to self-interested robins, who went about their business.

Networks and professional learning communities are flocks, but here the metaphor ends. The principle of flocking applies, but the conditions are very different for moral solutions involving deep learning, which is the case for educational reform. The downside includes the following.

First, educational ideas worth their salt are complex, not nearly as easy as learning how to pierce a milk top. Admittedly, networks are better than interruption strategies, at least for getting people's attention.

Second, quality knowledge is a key element of successful reform. Networks need to work hard at sorting out what are valuable and not-so-valuable ideas. Sometimes, beliefs, convictions, and groupthink subtly and not so subtly carry the day. At the very least, there is a large noise factor within any given network.

Third, and speaking of noise, when networks proliferate, ideas reign but coherence does not. When networks are embraced as a strategy, it is easy to think that you are pursuing complexity as you end up with clutter. Networks, by themselves, are not coherence-makers, despite the quotation earlier.

Fourth, and this is crucial with respect to moving forward: Networks do not have the line-authority for taking good ideas and creating the intense learning process that we know is essential for sustained implementation. Nor do they have the accountability legit-imacy for reinforcing and reporting on performance. Networks, how-ever, have the potential for contributing to focused implementation. The phenomenon of networks and collaboratives, of course, is not new. They have frequently existed as part of innovative strategies to access ideas—what is new is the deliberate attempt by the official system (governments) to employ networks as part of an integrated strategy for system reform.

None of this is to say throw the flock out. It argues for support-ing the lateral creativity and capacity-building potential of networks, as we worry about their limitations and build in mechanisms for inte-grating learning into sustained practice. We have already stressed the integrating roles of school leaders (Chapter 5) and district leaders (Chapter 6). Their role is to create learning communities within their organizations by learning from within, but also learning from and contributing to learning outside their jurisdictions. It is through the latter that people increase their system-thinking awareness and impact—an impact that is local and beyond.

GUIDELINES FOR SYSTEM LEADERS

Where does this leave us concerning the role of system leaders? This is precisely the question facing Michael Barber, Head of Prime

Minister Tony Blair's policy delivery unit, which oversees policy implementation in the areas of health, education, transportation, and crime. (How is that for a portfolio!) Barber is one of those new theoreticians to whom this book is devoted. Many of the ideas in this section are adapted from Barber and Fullan (2004), although I take full responsibility for the particular formulations here. There are 10 guidelines for system leaders committed to sustainability. These overlap with the eight elements of sustainability but are more customized to the system level agenda.

1. The reality test

2. Moral purpose

3. Get the basics right

4. Communicate the big picture

5. Provide opportunities for people to interact with the big picture

6. Intelligent accountability

7. Incentivize collaboration and lateral capacity building

8. The long lever of leadership

9. Design every policy, whatever the purpose, to build capacity, too

10. Grow the financial investment in education

1. The Reality Test

So far, system thinking has squandered its potential because it has stayed at the level of *thinking*. The reality test is to put it into practice. Because it has been missing from action, system thinking itself has remained stagnant. Good theories get better through continuous reflective action. Governments are always planning. They have a cadre of core staff constantly figuring out how to move ahead. The main message of this book is clear: Make system thinking and sustainability the agenda.

While previous chapters invite and provide ideas for other levels of the system, you cannot get very far if the system leaders themselves are not wanting to move in the same direction. The promise is that more will get done. And it may be good politics—getting results within one election period in order to go even further.

At a general level, this means that presidents, prime ministers, governors, premiers, and their staffs need to establish a coalition of leaders who are working toward greater capacity building. It will be hard and politically complex, but not abstract. Government leaders and staff could tackle the eight sustainability conditions in Chapter 2 in order to infuse policies and strategies in pursuit of educational reform. They could take the 10 lessons in this chapter and operationalize them. There is plenty of specificity in the ideas because they are all grounded in reality, one place or another.

There are some things we know and a host of unanswered questions, but this is the laboratory of the future. Like all good system thinking, it should be played out globally. As governments pursue this agenda, they have an obligation to learn from and contribute to others. Ontario, Canada, for example, is just launching into the sustainability agenda, and they are learning a lot from the British experience from the last 6 years. Their policies are being influenced by the lessons (the do's and the don'ts) of the Blair government's experiences over the past years. As Ontario's strategies evolve, the province will contribute back to the national and global scene. In the United States, several states that are being successful in improving literacy and numeracy can learn from each other as well as contribute more widely.

This whole book is about the tri-level solution—what has to happen at the school/community, district, and state levels. We are beginning to see more sophisticated thinking, policies, and strategies at the state level that focus on both capacity building and more effective accountability. I have referred to several examples with reference to England. The Premier of Ontario, Dalton McGuinty, just announced Ontario's main strategy for provincewide education change (McGunity, 2004). The strategy contains details of establishing a new Literacy and Numeracy Secretariat; funding the establishment of lead literacy and numeracy teachers in all 4,000 elementary schools; and training for schools, strategies for sharing best ideas, targets for dramatically improving student achievement, and a commitment to providing substantially more money (at a time of budget deficit) over the next 4 years. There will be more to the strategy as it evolves, and it is not yet a sustainability plan, but it is a significant step toward acknowledging that the state has a major responsibility to set the tone and direction for systemic change. The role of the state in focusing on viable strategies of reform is the least developed of the three levels and is the most significant in determining the chances for success.

Governments working in this way can pique each other's interests. Although a degree of humility will be in order, given the awesome nature of the task a little friendly competition has its place. How is each of us doing, for example, in the international comparisons conducted by the Organization for Economic Cooperation and Development (OECD)? Who is moving ahead, and how are they doing it? It is time to be transparent and engaged across borders.

Meanwhile, at home, the first reality test is to establish an overarching system model that contains a small number of interconnected priorities. Both the substance of the vision and the strategies about how to get there need to be defined and activated. A series of disconnected initiatives is not a system.

Beware of the trap of contrived coherence, where certain leaders can (or think they can) describe how the pieces fit in. This is not good enough. Such coherence may be only on paper, not in the reality of what the government actually does (as experienced by practitioners, for example). It may represent only potential coherence, where it really does have substance for some leaders, but not necessarily for those at the other levels. Most of the other nine guidelines work on the problem of connecting all levels to the bigger picture.

2. Moral Purpose

As my colleague Andy Hargreaves says, "System thinking has no morality" (personal communication). It can be used to mastermind a bank robbery, run organized crime, or eradicate certain ethnic groups. Moral purpose has a long tradition in education at the level of the individual teacher or principal. It is time to make it a system quality. Moral purpose is the link between system thinking and sustainability. You cannot move substantially toward sustainability in the absence of widely shared moral purpose. The reason is that sustainability depends on the distributed effort of people at all levels of the system, and meeting the goals of moral purpose produces commitment throughout the system.

Moral purpose, as we have discussed it, consists of raising the bar and closing the gap of student learning, treating people with demanding respect, and contributing to the social environment (e.g., other schools).

The pursuit of moral purpose must be relentless, because it can easily slip away. In light of the initial success in improving literacy and numeracy, Michael Barber urges new leaders not to let up. In a speech to consultant leaders (the strategy that links 1,000 lead primary principals successful in improving literacy with 4,000 other heads wanting to learn more), Barber (2004) identifies three risks for the next phase:

- Loss of momentum and focus on literacy and numeracy
- Seeing capacity building as long term, thereby losing the focus on short-term results
- Losing the precision of the definition of best practice in teaching

As Lesson 3 will say, we need to keep getting the basics right. We must and can focus simultaneously on short-term and long-term results. With networks and lateral capacity, we need to worry about what is best practice. In fact, we need to be both more precise about the basics and more precise about defining the deep learning we discussed via Claxton and others. The constant realization that this is a matter of moral purpose can provide the courage and commitment to keep going. This is relentless as a theme but must be punctuated by respites of cyclical-energizing rituals and periodic breaks (Chapter 2). As usual in system thinking, we need to worry about the too much/ too little problem. Too much moral purpose burns us out; too little leads to drift.

Let's also link the lessons. Terms travel easily; concepts don't. Moral purpose is becoming more and more popular. It is easy for articulate political leaders to co-opt the language but not the actions. Implementing the other nine lessons in the service of moral purpose makes this unlikely. System leaders need to model moral purpose in its own right and through the other strategies.

Finally, it is not just blatant immorality we need to worry about. Power is distributed unevenly in organizations and society, and it is not immediately apparent that those who currently benefit from greater privilege will be well served by raising the bar and closing the gap of student learning. As Kleiner (2003) so well argues, it is "the core group" in any organization or government *that really matters*. Kleiner notes that most organizations say the customer (or client, or student) comes first, but act to meet the needs of those in power.

The core group or coalition of leaders will always be there. Moral purpose means harnessing this power for what Kleiner (2003) calls a noble purpose:

> In organizations, honor has come to mean a sense of purpose that transcends merely "winning," "fulfilling the assignment," "making money," or "pleasing the core group." A truly honorable sense of purpose is one in which the organization seeks to leave the world a much better place, in some way closely related to the organization's own integrated learning base. (p. 217)

Sustainability means shifting the existing power base in school systems and ultimately in society. This is what makes it so hard. Yet the majority of people in most societies want greater moral purpose to permeate the workings of government. We need to elect governments who are serious about moral purpose, who constantly espouse it in the day-to-day reality of (in this case) working with school systems, and who draw it out and reward it until a critical mass of leaders is working together to create even more of it.

3. Get the Basics Right

The basics are literacy and numeracy in elementary and high schools. As Barber (2004) reports, despite a variety of reforms over the years, literacy performance in England remained stable for almost 50 years. One published report in 1995 reached the startling conclusion that the average levels of performance in literacy have remained much the same since 1948. The first thing that governments need to do is focus intensely on the basics to overcome the awful inertia of past decades. Governments need to prioritize and build a solid foundation as an essential start.

This need not be done with tunnel vision. We know that benefits in literacy and numeracy flow to other cognitive areas, such as science. With a little effort, they benefit laterally to the arts and drama. As the work unfolds, one can get more and more ambitious about the connections. Doing the basics is never-ending; doing them better and deep is the goal. The agenda for the immediate future includes the following:

1. Raise the floor in literacy and numeracy in those schools, districts, states, and countries where performance is unacceptably low.

2. Raise the bar and close the gap, and when levels of performance improve, keep going toward proficiency levels that are in the 90% range.

3. Make sure that literacy (English) and numeracy (the maths) are equally pursued in middle and high schools—otherwise, early gains will be lost.

4. Use increasingly powerful strategies so that literacy and numeracy are used in the service of deep learning (Claxton's, 2002, "building learning power," for example).

The unfolding of the basics is not without its controversy, so keep the channels open and the debate alive. Can some forms of teaching literacy and numeracy raise test scores but turn students off learning? Can targets dominate in unhelpful ways? Is there sufficient attention to capacity building? How do you keep a relentless focus on the basics when there are many competing priorities? Whatever— but if you don't get the basics right, there is little foundation for doing all the other things that matter.

4. Communicate the Big Picture

Assuming the big picture is coherent (Lesson 1), driven by moral purpose (2), and prioritized (3), system leaders must become preoccupied with communicating the overall purpose and plan. A perennial complaint that locals have is that they don't understand "the big picture." Put positively, when local leaders do connect with larger-system purposes, they are much more effective within their own organizations and certainly across organizations when they step out.

The advice to system leaders is to communicate, communicate, communicate. Written words are not enough. Lots of interaction will be required. There are two purposes to these exchanges. One is that good system leaders will have a lot to say, and it helps enormously if leaders are transparent, coherent, and inspiring about the short- and long-term purposes of reform. The second purpose is that leaders learn to sharpen and refine the message as they are pushed to become clearer and to take into account objections and suggestions from the field. If they are connected with practice, they also discover examples of local success that connect to the bigger picture.

This has aspects of top-downness in the sense that system leaders forcefully present a compelling agenda, but it is shaped and reshaped because leaders with system thinking act in ways that bring them close to the problems on many occasions. Some of the other lessons. such as lateral capacity building and leadership development, provide additional checks to undue dominance from the center.

There are at least three audiences at play, with the format for communication different in each case. One is the general public, so that legitimacy, accountability, and related feedback are processed, especially critical vis-à-vis Lesson 10. The second is special interest groups (special education associations, teacher unions, administrator councils, labor and business leaders, and so on). The third concerns local practitioners, superintendents, principals, and teachers, who are the frontline agents of success or failure.

5. Opportunities for Locals to Influence the Big Picture

Part of this activity occurs in the previous lesson. As system leaders communicate, they are being influenced by the responses they receive. Here, I am talking about something more explicit. The hypothesis is that as locals understand and identify with the big picture, they increase their system-thinking capacity, which is part and parcel of system change. To do this requires three interrelated activities: (1) putting the content and underlying principles and strategies out there for public consumption; (2) establishing learning opportunities for interaction around the plans for people to internalize the deeper meaning of the plans (it is especially important that people see their roles in the context of a bigger agenda and not just as a fragmented cog); and (3) providing periodic occasions where plans are assessed and reviewed in order to generate recommendations for revising policies and strategies.

All of this is critical for what we have called "adaptive challenges." where the solutions are not known and where progress depends on joint commitment and ownership. In the systems we are talking about, this works better because there is plenty of interaction going on (within and across the three levels of school and community/ district/and state). It works also because the redefinition of local roles (school and district) includes the invitation, expectation, and corresponding resources to step out and participate in the bigger system (see Chapters 5 and 6). Once this is under way, the number of connection points that "naturally" occur is greatly increased and may exponentially spread, akin to the "idea virus" metaphor mentioned at the outset of this chapter.

6. Intelligent Accountability

"Intelligent accountability" is a phrase used by David Miliband (2004), Minister of State for School Standards in England. Of course, any leader, not the least a minister of state, would consider his or her approach to accountability to be "intelligent." But we have something else to go on: It's called *evidence.* The area of accountability will always be contentious, but the debate can be greatly sharpened by examining what is working best.

Two things—somewhat at odds, but not fatally so—have to be accomplished. One involves transparent, external accountability to the public and to the government as the public's agency (sometimes called "assessment of learning" or "summative assessment"); the other concerns the use of data on student learning as a strategy for directly improving teaching and learning (called "assessment for learning" or "formative assessment").

Governments typically overemphasize assessment of learning at the expense of assessment for learning. Teacher unions do the opposite. There may be grounds for agreement as this particular adaptive challenge gets addressed. Virtually everyone agrees that new capacities for assessment for learning on the part of teachers, schools, and districts are essential, high-yield strategies, but as we have seen, the area of assessment remains contentious (see Association of Teachers and Lecturers, National Union of Teachers, and Professional Association of Teachers, 2004, for a union perspective).

Moreover, the methodology for developing this capacity is increasingly specific. Work by Black et al. (2002); Hill and Crevola (2003); and Stiggins (2001) is particularly helpful. As far as our "new theoreticians" are concerned, there are now scores of teacher leaders, principals, and district staff, with whom we and others are working, who are increasingly proficient at "collective" versions (professional learning communities) of assessment for learning. Lateral capacity strategies beckon!

Second, governments directly and indirectly do have a moral obligation to intervene in cases of persistently poor performance. Our view is that when they do intervene, they should do so rarely, do it well, actively involve expert practitioners, and draw powerfully on the evidence base (Barber & Fullan, 2004). To intervene, they have to know the evidence base.

Third, integrating assessment of and for learning may be the best approach. The dual goal is to increase capacity as you assure and inform the public.

Reified targets are a problem; so is "annual yearly progress," as used in the No Child Left Behind policy in the United States. But then again, so is bowing to professional autonomy. This much is clear: Work at all levels to infuse the system with excellent data (not reams of information) and ensure that school and district staff have the capacity to use the data so that everyone knows what affect the staff's actions are having on student learning. And then, make adjustments with respect to what is working. System development occurs not just when good data are available, but when people agree on the meaning and use of the data.

7. Incentivize Collaboration and Lateral Capacity Building

You can't develop systems directly. You have to use the system to develop itself. Again, we have a high-yield strategy. Invest a little to help leaders to lead beyond their schools, and reap the benefit. I have given many examples throughout the book of what this looks like in practice and have commented at the beginning of this chapter on the limitations of this strategy by itself. Some forms of lateral capacity building occur within the school or within the district. These are the responsibility of school and district leaders. System leaders can establish explicit expectations that these kinds of intraorganizational, professional-learning communities are deep and valuable.

Beyond this, system leaders have a special responsibility to foster and support cross-system networks, where people across a region, state, or country learn from each other. When done well, this has multiple payoffs for our system sustainability agenda. First, people get access to good ideas from other practitioners—ideas that are grounded and workable from respected peers who have successfully grappled with difficult problems. Second, people begin to identify with larger parts of the system beyond their narrow interest groups. We have seen it time and again in our work. When people get out to do something worthwhile with peers in other schools or jurisdictions, the sense of community and commitment enlarges. One's identity to a larger common purpose amplifies. Third, if enough people get out where "system concerns" form the substance of the exchanges—such as the content of the previous six elements, for example—the collective capacity to system think, and thus to system change, is advanced.

It is important that collaboration and networking, as I have said, are not pursued as ends seen as automatically good in and of themselves. Like each of the 10 elements here, they must be crafted and assessed as part of a complex of forces that creates new synergies that enhance the continuing performance of the system as a whole.

8. The Long Lever of Leadership

The title of this book says that the longest lever we have at our disposal is leadership: leadership at all levels, leaders who leave behind a legacy of leaders who can go even farther, leadership succession that provides continuity of good direction, leaders who step out to make wider contributions, and a pipeline of leaders developing their dispositions and skills well before they take their first full-time formal positions of authority.

An important but partial aspect of this strategy involves establishing standards and related qualifications frameworks that potential leaders must meet in order to be certified or qualified for leadership positions. These standards can orient leaders in the right direction and give them individual experiences and development. They suffer from what I call the "individualistic bias." The assumption is that if you produce enough individual leaders with the new desired characteristics, then the system will change. Not so. Systems quickly blunt or socialize new members. This is why we need to work simultaneously on individual development and system change.

A second matter is that the new standards are likely biased toward what Heifetz (2004) called "technical solutions"—important ones, such as improving literacy and numeracy, but not the tough ones concerning adaptive challenges.

Third, and in addition to strengthening qualifications frameworks, systems can stress leadership development, provide support for leadership councils, and fund and endorse leadership growth through lateral capacity-building projects. What system leaders should want to see is the proliferation of leadership of the kind I identified in Chapters 4 through 6, where the lead leaders are creating intensive opportunities for new leaders *to learn in context*—job-embedded learning that is specific to the organization and is learned on the job through mentoring and related opportunities to engage in reflective practice, working with others on significant school and district priorities. This learning in context can be widened so that the context is other schools in the district and beyond.

Fourth, and I do not have the space to do this justice, the revamping of the teaching profession should be designed to provide expectations and opportunities for every teacher to become a leader from day 1 on the job (and before during teacher preparation). Teachers' experience during the first 5 to 7 years of teaching determines the quality and quantity of the pool of future leaders.

Most strategists now recommend that organizations invest in generating a continuous, broad-based *pool* of leaders rather than particular earmarked succession leaders. This is consistent with the above points. Every teacher is a leader, and the more that leadership is fostered for everyone, the larger the natural system pool. Incidentally, these ideas apply to district level strategies as well as system level sponsorship. Two recent books with almost identical titles capture this new emphasis. Fulmer and Conger's (2004) *Growing Your Company's Leaders* says that the old way was to identify replacements for senior executives, and "companies rarely considered the possibility that it might be deployed for genuine development or for retention of talented individuals" (p. 4). The new way is developmentally oriented.

Byham, Smith, and Paese's (2002) *Grow Your Own Leaders* makes a similar argument. Most companies lose talent because they fail to provide opportunities for "personal growth and job challenges" (p. 1). They advocate the "acceleration pool" approach, which is "more developmental," "more involving," "more flexible," and "more tailored to specific organization situations and needs" (p. ii).

We already know that searching for external savior leaders hardly produces short-term results and is dysfunctional for sustainability. Business books advocate internal development of leaders for competitive edges: cultivate, retain, and promote your own talent for the betterment of the firm. My argument favors the moral edge as well. Promote good leadership in all quarters of the system, and everyone will be better off. So what if you cultivate great leaders and other schools and districts pick off your trained talent? If you are that good an employer, other systems will pale by comparison. Just as MIT has recently made all of its courses available free on-line because they know they are in a bigger game, systems need to make all of their talent available. Get better at a good game, contribute to the overall good, and be a sustainable winner in the process. "What goes around comes around" applies to good things as well as bad things.

9. Design Every Policy, Whatever the Purpose, to Build Capacity, Too

There is a major trap that system leaders fall into: They assume or are oblivious to whether capacity to implement given policies automatically follows the introduction of supposedly good practice. Here, the lesson is, don't invest a lot of money up front if the capacity to use it effectively is missing. It is better to evolve the money. Let money follow capacity as much as it promotes it.

The more positive version is to do some deep soul-searching before proposing and implementing a new policy on the questions of: What capacities would it take to implement this policy? To what extent do these capacities exist in the system? And how can we promote greater capacity in the course of implementation? The natural bias of policymakers is toward short-term accountability rather than mid- or long-term capacity building. System leaders interested in sustainability need to balance short- and long-term outcomes. They need to play down their tendency to answer immediate accountability questions in favor of promoting new skills and dispositions.

Every new policy, then, is an occasion to question and promote greater capacity in the system. There is no point in advocating new policies if you are not at the same time promoting the capacities necessary to implement the policies in practice. So, the proposal is to constantly assess capacity and promote it on every occasion. Every policy can be scrutinized from the point of view as to whether it contributes to short- and long-term results.

Accountability concerns come easy to system leaders; capacity building does not. System leaders need to invest in capacity building because it does not come naturally and the payoff can be considerable. When new strategies link kindred spirits already moving in this direction, they can catapult forward. System level thinkers grow the future by coupling each and every new policy with the question: What will it take for the system to have the capacity to be successful at implementing this policy? Accountability and capacity go hand in hand in sustainable societies, and you have to invest equally in each.

10. Grow the Financial Investment in Education

Some new investment is needed up front, but after that, this year's success is next year's new money. The public potentially wants to invest more in education because they intuitively know that more education means more prosperity and well-being for everyone. But they are not confident that the investment will yield results. The new system thinkers are pleased to enter the quid pro quo world of delivering results for more resources. They are willing to take the risks and to make the extra effort on the promise that success breeds success.

Sustainability is resource generative and resource hungry. However, the resources in question are not simply add-on costs. When goodwill is low, every solution costs money because people will not put in the extra effort. When goodwill gains momentum, resources are not just money but also effort, energy, and inventiveness. In all respects, sustainability requires new investments, but its momentum produces more than it consumes new resources.

The culmination of the previous nine lessons in action is greater investment in the future of sustainability. It may not represent largesse in the short run, but the direction will be unmistakable. The nemesis of sustainability in the physical environment involves the conspicuous consumption of irreplaceable resources. The beauty of positive social forces is that they produce self-generating resources. Existing resources are used with greater focus, and, in turn, success attracts additional investments. It is about working smarter, not just harder; but it is also about accruing well-deserved resources that enable us to go deeper and further. The ultimate satisfaction is the realization that the public wants to invest even more in the future—a natural outgrowth of sustainable actions converging.

There you have it. Politicians and policymakers need to model new theoreticians in action, and create the conditions for others around them and through the system to get better at it. They need to deliver on short-term results as they pave the way for longer-term sustainability. If they can get this balancing act together, they will become more politically attractive, which allows them to do even more. Old system-thinking politicians in action never die, because they leave such a legacy.

Epilogue
It's Going to Be Hard

Moral purpose, changing context, lateral capacity building, intelligent accountability, deep learning, short-term and long-term results, cyclical energizing, the long lever of leadership: It all sounds so damn virtuous and irresistible. Try it, and you will find that the forces are not with you. Why? If we integrate the insights of Perkins (2003) and Heifetz and Linsky (2002), we can see how hard this job of paving the way for sustainability is going to be. (The quoted material in this section comes from these two sources.)

Perkins (2003), it will be recalled, says that for systems to be habitually smart, they have to dramatically increase the number of "progressive interactions" and minimize the amount of "regressive interactions." Progressive interactions maximize quality knowledge and social cohesion. He calls these two aspects "process smart" (good exchange of ideas, good decisions and solutions, farseeing plans) and "people smart" (interactions that foster cohesiveness and energize people to work together). Our previous three chapters are about leadership at the school, district, and system levels that are process- and people-smart. They are not the norm. Regressive interactions don't get at ideas, or do so poorly; plans don't get made, or followed if they do; people are dissatisfied, at loggerheads, or opt out because it is easier to do so. There is more regression than progression in daily life.

System or organizational intelligence is very hard to come by, says Perkins (2003), for at least six big reasons:

1. *The five brain backlash*—too many voices making things unproductively complicated;

2. *Cognitive oversimplification*—the human tendency to over-simplify cognitive processing;

3. *Emotional oversimplification*—the equally human tendency to oversimplify emotions;

4. *Regression in the face of stress;*

5. *The domino effect* in which one person's regressive behavior tips others in the same direction; and

6. Power advantage—the fact that power figures sometimes take advantage of regressive interactions. (p. 75; his emphasis)

There is one overriding reason why regressive interactions are more likely to happen and to have staying power. They are easier to do. It is easier to opt out of a bad process than to try to correct it. It is easier to give someone superficial or no feedback or even negative feedback than to engage in the progressive interactions of effective feedback. It is less trouble to sweep conflict under the carpet than to confront it. It is safer not to count on people than to be disappointed. It is simpler to make decisions alone than with others. It is even easier to hate than to love, because you can hate all by yourself. You can hate by stereotype, but you must love by involvement. In short, regressive behavior is easier because you can do it all by yourself; progressive behavior is harder because you have to do it with others at a time that you don't feel like cooperating.

So, regressive interactions are much simpler, with the payoff immediate, while progressive interactions must be carefully woven over time, with the hypothetical payoff down the road. Progressive interactions are more complicated to establish and maintain because they require people to stay engaged over long periods of time. Perkins (2003) says that both regressive and progressive archetypes of interactions stimulate their own, but regressive ones are more likely to spread because they are simpler. Progressive interactions are more sophisticated and complex and therefore less likely to catch on; they "are less stable than regressive ones [and thus] require deliberate commitment, effort and vigilance on the part of leaders and participants" (p. 125).

Stated in our terms, even when sustainability (which is progressive) is on the move, it is less stable than stubborn regression. They don't call it "inertia" for nothing.

As if this is not enough bad news, *under stressful conditions, individuals and groups are more likely to revert to regressive behavior.* Some stress, as we have seen, is essential as part and parcel of pushing into new frontiers, but too much stress can cause us to seize up, get angry, and get even more frustrated with the complexities of group deliberations and thus to withdraw from the fray.

Tackling complex adaptive challenges increases stress (Heifetz calls it "disequilibrium"). Thus precisely when the group needs to be at its progressive best is the most likely time it will revert to regressive habits.

We can recall some of the key properties of adaptive challenges identified by Heifetz and Linsky (2002): Adaptive challenges require new learning beyond our existing capacities; there will be loss as well as potential gain; losses involve learning to refashion loyalties and develop new competencies; adaptive work requires longer time frames, and so on. Adaptive challenges present an invitation to deep new learning, but they are also occasions for Perkins's (2003) six barriers to raise their ugly heads.

Heifetz and Linsky (2002) underscore the difficulties by observing that

> To lead is to live dangerously because when leadership counts, when you lead people through difficult change, you challenge what people hold dear—their daily habits, tools, loyalties, and ways of thinking—with nothing more to offer perhaps than a possibility. . . . People push back when you disturb the personal and institutional equilibrium they know. And people resist in all kinds of creative and unexpected ways that can get you taken out of the game: pushed aside, undermined, or eliminated. (p. 2)

And remember, it takes less skill to resist than to learn. Resistance comes naturally; learning complicated things in a group setting does not. It is easy for people to avoid or fail to persist in the deep, cognitive, emotional, and political learning cycles that will be needed to sustain the group's focus on complex new challenges.

I say all of this not so that would-be system thinkers should pack their bags and go home. Just the opposite—so they know realistically what they are up against and then can take the practical steps to make success more likely. We don't need leaders who get good at a bad game by becoming experts at self-serving regressive behaviors. And we don't need leaders who are morally right, only to blame the system for not seeing the value and wisdom of their ways.

So, let's start with the stark realism that the work of sustainability is going to be very hard to do, with lots of backward steps along the way. After that, the question is: How can our new theoreticians in action learn to live dangerously, just enough to get breakthroughs but not enough to get destroyed? There are many answers to this question throughout the book, but let's put them in perspective here.

The general response is to get a team of leaders around you and map out a strategy and approach that implements the eight elements of sustainability in Chapter 2. This is not as abstract as it sounds, because those interested in system change are not starting from scratch. But we can do better than this.

Leadership is sometimes touted for its altruistic value of making lives better for people around you. To me, it is unlikely that this moral motivation will carry the day in facing down regressive resistance. Commitment to the larger good is one key, but it is not sufficient. The attraction for the new theoreticians is the cognitive and emotional challenge of cracking a complex set of problems and doing something good in the process. The long lever of leadership is a lightning rod (pardon the mixed metaphor) for leaders who can't resist what Perkins (2003) calls "action poetry." To repeat his definition:

The language of real change needs not just explanation theories, or even action theories, but good action poetry—action theories that are built for action—simple, memorable, and evocative. (p. 213)

The call, then, is for developmental leaders (system thinkers in action) who do not stand back and conduct passive analysis, but because of their immersion and system perspectives learn to size up situations quickly and intuitively, using the concepts discussed in this book. Developmental leaders, according to Perkins (2003), have "a receptive alertness" (p. 217). These new leaders adopt progressive practices "regardless of what others are doing" (p. 217) and "function as exemplars, facilitators and mentors within a group, helping to move it toward a progressive culture" (p. 219). The long lever of leadership acts in a way to create a culture of many leaders who rub off on each other in the new direction, explicitly eschewing regressive practices. This intensive work, as we have seen, does not pay off overnight: "The true harvest of all this comes not from the particular occasion but the long-term effects" (p. 218).

I have also said that it is impossible to get a system perspective if you only stay at home. Like the titmice example, leaders need to mix and match inside their organizations and in external (purposeful) networks. We need cross-connected leadership experiences literally in order to broaden people's horizons. A critical mass of such leaders throughout the system can eventually cause the system itself to transform so that progressive cultures flourish.

Heifetz and Linsky (2002) have a number of more specific suggestions exactly in line with the theme of leadership and sustainability. One is "staying on the balcony and being on the dance floor" almost simultaneously. The dance floor is the intense leadership for deep learning. The balcony is standing back to get perspective, and visiting other settings where you can observe from a distance. Practice moving back and forth, being in the midst of the trees while you alternatively get a view of the whole forest.

Another practical but sophisticated strategy from Heifetz and Linsky (2002) is close to our cyclical-energy concept: Control the temperature and pace of work. Energy, not time, is the key to sustainability. Sometimes adaptive challenges require a push for more energy because there is not enough press on the problem; on other occasions, people need a time-out because things are boiling over or people are getting spent. If focus is low, Heifetz and Linsky (2002) recommend "raising the temperature" by "drawing attention to the tough questions," "giving people more responsibility than they are comfortable with," "bringing conflicts to the surface," and "protecting gadflies and oddballs" (p. 111).

If things are too intense, we can slow down by "addressing the technical aspects of the problem," "establishing a structure for the problem-solving process by breaking the problem into parts and creating timeframes," "reclaiming [as leader] responsibility for tough issues," and "slowing down the process of challenging norms and expectations" (p. 111).

The same with the pace of change. Sometimes, it is important not to take on yet another priority no matter how attractive it may be. The new work of developmental leaders involves inviting the people with the problems to be the solution shapers. This requires pace, cultivation of leadership in others, soaking up the possibilities, and extracting and consolidating gains. As a recent commercial says, "The race between art and science ends in a tie." This is the new theoretician in a nutshell.

The reason that new leadership is required is that the breakthroughs we have been addressing in this book are very "hard to do." Ordinarily, leadership gets competence at best. What we need is leadership that motivates people to take on the complexities and anxieties of difficult change. The new theoretician makes this extra-ordinary work possible. When the conditions of sustainability are put in place, the work is more efficient, effective, and rewarding. We need systems of people who are willing to go the extra mile, partly because the cause is noble, but also because they experience and know that success is possible.

From a system perspective, the single answer to the question of how to increase the chances for greater sustainability is to build a critical mass of developmental leaders who can mix and match, and who can surround themselves with other leaders across the system as they spread the new leadership capacities to others. Adaptive challenges such as sustainability, moral purpose for all, deep learning, fine-tuning intelligent accountability, productive lateral capacity building, and getting results never before attained can be tremendously enticing once you start to get good at doing them. People find meaning by connecting to others; and they find well-being by making progress on problems important to their peers and of benefit beyond themselves.

It has always been hard enough to be good at theory or good at practice. Sustainability is asking for more: system thinkers in action who don't thrive in armchairs or in trenches are at their best when they are on the dance floor and the balcony on the same day. There is nothing so theoretical as applied practice in addressing complex problems. There is nothing more satisfying than seeing hordes of people engaged to do good together because of the leadership you helped produce.

Mission impossible? Maybe. But don't give it another armchair thought. To the new theoretician, mission impossible is just another hypothesis to be tested. Go for it.

References

Ackerman, M., Pipek, V., & Wulf, V. (Eds.). (2003). *Sharing expertise: Beyond knowledge management*. Cambridge: MIT Press.

Association of Teachers and Lecturers, National Union of Teachers, and Professional Association of Teachers. (2004). *Reclaiming assessment for teaching and learning*. London: Author.

Barber, M. (2002, April 23). *From good to great: Large-scale reform in England*. Paper presented at Futures of Education Conference, Universität Zürich, Zürich.

Barber, M. (2004). *Courage and the lost art of bicycle maintenance*. London: Consultants Conference.

Barber, M., & Fullan, M. (2004). *Recent lessons for system reform*. Submitted for publication.

Bentley, T. (2003). Foreword. In D. Hargreaves, *Education epidemic*. London: Demos.

Bentley, T., & Wilsdon, J. (2003). *The adaptive state*. London: Demos.

Bereiter, C. (2002). *Education and mind in the knowledge age*. Mahwah, NJ: Lawrence Erlbaum.

Black, P., Harrison, C., Lee, C., Marshall, B., & Wiliam, D. (2003). *Assessment for learning*. Philadelphia: Open University Press.

Blanchard, J. (2002). *Teaching and targets*. New York: RoutledgeFalmer.

Block, P. (1987). *The empowered manager*. San Francisco: Jossey-Bass.

Brighouse, T., & Woods, D. (1999). *How to improve your school*. London: Routledge.

Bryk, A., & Schneider, B. (2002). *Trust in schools*. New York: Russell Sage Foundation.

Byham, W., Smith, A., & Paese, M. (2002). *Grow your own leaders*. Englewood Cliffs, NJ: Financial Times, Prentice Hall.

Chapman, J. (2003). Public value. In T. Bentley & J. Wilsdon (Eds.), *The adaptive state*. London: Demos.

Claxton, G. (2002). *Building learning power*. Bristol, UK: Henleaze House.

Collins, J. (2001). *Good to great*. New York: HarperCollins.

Council of Chief School Officers. (2002). *Expecting success: A study of five high performing, high poverty schools*. Washington, DC: Author.

DeGues, A. (1997). *The living company.* Cambridge, MA: Harvard Business School Press.

Deming, W. E. (1986). *Out of the crisis.* Cambridge: MIT Press.

Department for Education and Skills. (2004). *Results of school reform in England.* London: Author.

Earl, L., Levin, B., Leithwood, K., Fullan, M., & Watson, N. (2003). *Watching and learning 3.* London: Department for Education and Skills.

Farson, R., & Keyes, R. (2002). *Whoever makes the most mistakes wins.* New York: Free Press.

Flintham, A. (2003). *When reservoirs run dry.* Nottingham, UK: National College for School Leaders.

Fullan, M. (2001). *Leading in a culture of change.* San Francisco: Jossey-Bass.

Fullan, M. (2003a). *Change forces with a vengeance.* London: RoutledgeFalmer.

Fullan, M. (2003b). *The moral imperative of school leadership.* Thousand Oaks, CA: Corwin.

Fullan, M. (2004). *Whole system reform.* Paper prepared for New American Schools, Arlington, VA.

Fullan, M., Bertani, A., & Quinn, J. (2004). Lessons from district-wide reform. *Educational Leadership, 61*(6).

Fullan, M., & Hargreaves, A. (1992). *What's worth fighting for in your school.* New York: Teachers College Press.

Fulmer, R., & Conger, J. (2004). *Growing your company's leaders.* New York: AMACOM Books.

Gladwell, M. (2000). *The tipping point.* Boston: Little, Brown.

Godin, S. (2001). *Unleashing the idea virus.* New York: Do You Zoom.

Goleman, D., Boyatzis, R., & McKee, A. (2002). *Primal leadership.* Boston: Harvard Business School Press.

Hargreaves, A. (2002). Teaching and betrayal. *Teachers and Teaching, 8*(3/4).

Hargreaves, A. (2004). *The carousel of leadership succession.* Submitted for publication.

Hargreaves, A., & Fink, D. (2000, April). The three dimensions of reform. *Educational leadership,* 30–34.

Hargreaves, A., & Fink, D. (in press). *Sustainable leadership.* San Francisco: Jossey-Bass.

Hargreaves, A., Moore, S., Fink, D., Brayman, C., & White, R. (2003). *Succeeding leaders.* Toronto, Canada: Ontario Principals Council.

Hargreaves, D. (2003). *Education epidemic.* London: Demos.

Hartle, F., & Thomas, K. (2003). *Growing school leaders: The challenge.* Nottingham, UK: National College of School Leaders.

Hay Group Management Ltd. (2004). *A culture for learning.* London: Author.

Heifetz, R. (2003). Adaptive work. In T. Bentley & J. Wilsdon (Eds.), *The adaptive state* (pp. 68–78). London: Demos.

Heifetz, R. (2004, February 1). *The adaptive challenge.* Presentation to the American Association of School Administrators, San Francisco.

Heifetz, R., & Linsky, M. (2002). *Leadership on the line: Staying alive through the dangers of leading.* Boston: Harvard Business School Press.

Hill, P., & Crevola, C. (2003). *From a school based to a system based approach to balanced literacy.* Paper presented at Quest Conference, York Region, Toronto, Canada.

Hopkins, D. (2001). *School improvement for real.* London: Routledge-Falmer.

Kegan, R., & Lahey, L. (2001). *How the way we talk can change the way we work.* San Francisco: Jossey Bass.

Khurana, R. (2002). *Searching for a corporate savior: The irrational quest for charismatic CEOs.* Princeton, NJ: Princeton University Press.

Kleiner, A. (2003). *What really matters.* New York: Doubleday.

Loehr, J., & Schwartz, T. (2003). *The power of full engagement.* New York: Free Press.

Macbeath, J., Schratz, M., Meuret, D., & Jakobsen, L. (2000). *Self evaluation in European schools.* London: RoutledgeFalmer.

McGuinty, D. (2004, April 22). Speech to the Character Education Conference, York Region, Ontario, Canada.

Miliband, D. (2004, January 8). *Personalized learning: Building new relationships with schools.* Speech presented to the North of England Education Conference, Belfast, Northern Ireland.

Munby, S. (2003). *Broad and deep: A whole authority approach to motivation and learning.* Mersey, UK: Knowsley Local Education Authority.

National College of School Leadership. (2003a). *Like no other initiative.* Nottingham, UK: Author.

National College of School Leadership. (2003b). *Why networked learning communities.* Nottingham, UK: Author.

National Research Council. (1999). *How people learn.* Washington, DC: National Academy Press.

Noguera, P. (2003). *City schools and the American dream.* New York: Teachers College Press.

Office for Standards in Education (OFSTED). (2003a). *Inspection report: Knowsley Local Education Authority.* London: Author.

Office for Standards in Education (OFSTED). (2003b). *Leadership and management: Managing the school workforce.* London: Author.

Office for Standards in Education (OFSTED). (2003c). *Leadership and management: What inspection tells us.* London: Author.

Ouchi, W. (2003). *Making schools work.* New York: Wiley.

Perkins, D. (2003). *King Arthur's roundtable.* New York: Wiley.

Pfeffer, J., & Sutton, R. (2000). *The knowing-doing gap: How smart companies turn knowledge into action.* Boston: Harvard Business School Press.

Popham, J. (2004). *America's "failing schools": How parents and teachers can cope with No Child Left Behind.* New York: RoutledgeFalmer.

Reina, D., & Reina, M. (1999). *Trust and betrayal in the workplace.* San Francisco: Berrett Koehler.

Roza, M. (2003). *A matter of definition: Is there really a shortage of school principals?* New York: Wallace Foundation.

Scott, G. (2003). *Learning principals.* Sydney, Australia: University of Technology.

Senge, P. (1990). *The fifth discipline.* New York: Doubleday.

Senge, P., Cambron McCabe, N., Lucas, T., Smith, B., Dutton, J., & Kleiner, A. (2000). *Schools that learn.* New York: Doubleday.

Snipes, J., Doolittle, F., & Herlihy, P. (2002). *Foundations for success.* Washington, DC: Council of the Great City Schools.

Stiggins, R. (2001). *Student involved classroom assessment* (3rd ed.). Ohio: Merrill Prentice Hall.

Stoll, L., & Fink, D. (2002). *It's about learning: It's about time.* London: RoutledgeFalmer.

Storr, A. (1988). *Solitude.* London: Flamingo Press.

Togneri, W., & Anderson, S. (2003). How high poverty districts improve. *Educational Leadership, 33*(1), 12–17.

Wallace Foundation. (2003). *Beyond the pipeline.* New York: Author.

Williams, T. (2001). *Unrecognized exodus.* Toronto, Canada: Ontario Principals' Council.

Index

**CORWIN
PRESS**

The Corwin Press logo—a raven striding across an open book—represents the union of courage and learning. Corwin Press is committed to improving education for all learners by publishing books and other professional development resources for those serving the field of K–12 education. By providing practical, hands-on materials, Corwin Press continues to carry out the promise of its motto: **"Helping Educators Do Their Work Better."**

O N T A R I O
PRINCIPALS'
C O U N C I L
Exemplary Leadership
in Public Education

The Ontario Principals' Council (OPC) is a voluntary professional association for principals and vice-principals in Ontario's public school system. We believe that exemplary leadership results in outstanding schools and improved student achievement. To this end, we foster quality leadership through world-class professional services and supports. As an ISO 9001 registered organization, we are committed to our statement that "quality leadership is our principal product."